The Citadel of *Awareness*

The Citadel of *Awareness*

A Commentary on
Jigme Lingpa's Dzogchen Aspiration Prayer

Anam Thubten

The Citadel of Awareness

A Commentary on
Jigme Lingpa's Dzogchen Aspiration Prayer
By Anam Thubten

Third Edition

Cover image of Jigme Lingpa © Dharmata Foundation
Cover design by Anne McLellan

ISBN: 978-1-7320208-4-9

Table of Contents

Editor's Note

In the winter of 2020, much of the world was locked down as people everywhere grappled with the effects of a pandemic, then in its sixth month, with no clear end in sight. At the same time that many outer activities ceased, online events blossomed. In the midst of this, Anam Thubten began work on his commentary on Jigme Lingpa's *Dzogchen Aspiration Prayer*. Taking advantage of technology, he and I used online video conferencing to work together, resulting in this book, which surprisingly was completed more quickly than any of the previous books we had produced. Our "virtual" work together became a joyous venture—to ease video fatigue, we took frequent chai breaks, had time for laughter, and made sure to get up and stretch regularly.

Yet despite this modern modality, there was something ancient about the process. The Tibetan Buddhist tradition that Anam Thubten comes from has historically been an oral tradition. The Buddhist sutras often begin with "Thus have I heard..." The ancient masters revealed sacred scriptures by speaking them aloud to disciples who transcribed them by hand. This book was created in a similar way, as an oral transmission. Anam Thubten would read a verse by Jigme Lingpa and then, with seemingly little effort, begin a commentary on it while I typed what he said. He explained

Dzogchen terms, complex philosophy, and practical applications without relying on notes or preparing his words in advance. Occasionally, we would pause as he researched a quote or read texts by Dzogchen masters from the past. Much as a "pen does not know what it is writing," my fingers didn't really know what I was typing. Yet when we both returned to read the manuscript, it was astoundingly complete, needing very little revision.

Editing Conventions

Since the book emerged from an oral process, a number of editing decisions were made. One was to intersperse headings to break up what was actually an uninterrupted flow of words. Occasionally, it was possible to use a line of the verse itself as a heading. However, that was not always the case, as Anam Thubten spoke extemporaneously from start to finish on each verse, sometimes coming back to the verse, but at other times taking his own direction on what was important to emphasize.

Another editing decision was to leave much of the cadence and flow of Anam Thubten's voice throughout the text rather than edit the content into a more formal, written style. Often, Anam Thubten uses multiple words or phrases to describe a single concept, which creates a melodic or poetic style to his teaching. In addition, in keeping with the nonconceptual approach of Dzogchen, this creates a spaciousness around concepts, allowing for a multiplicity of meanings to take the reader beyond the concept itself.

At one point in the book, Anam Thubten offers this suggestion to readers: "Whenever someone wants to study these things, it is important to bear in mind that one cannot be too rational or logical; otherwise, these teachings won't be approachable. The reader should remember that they have to be read from a different state of mind." I encourage readers to take his words to heart, and let the contents of this book wash over you in a nonconceptual way.

Acknowledgements

I would like to express my gratitude to Catherine Hollander, Laura Kurtzman, Ruvain Gittelman, and Liane Allahdadi for reviewing the manuscript and catching multiple typos. Any remaining errors are fully my own responsibility. Thank you also to Anne McLellan who designed the cover and assisted with layout decisions. My utmost gratitude goes to Anam Thubten, who poured out these teachings from his heart, then meticulously reread them word by word to ensure that this book represents his meaning.

Note on Foreign Languages

Throughout his teaching, Anam Thubten often uses Tibetan words or phrases, which he then translates into English. In many cases, we have kept the Tibetan. The style we use is to include phonetics followed by Wylie transliteration in parentheses. While Anam Thubten's pronunciation is a Tibetan dialect from Golok, in this text we are using phonetics for the commonly known Lhasa pronunciation. For Sanskrit terms, we have omitted diacriticals, adding an "h" after "s" or "c" when the pronunciation requires it. In general, only the first occurrence of any foreign word is italicized.

Laura Duggan

AUTHOR'S PREFACE

Many people today, in both the East and the West, are becoming fascinated with Dzogchen. Yet there have always been people throughout history with a great interest in nondual teachings. There are two reasons for this. One is that they have the mindset that can capture these kinds of profound teachings. Another reason is that people are really longing for liberation and are secretly tired of endless spiritual practice. They just want to wake up right now. Dzogchen is one of those teachings that promises that awakening can happen in this lifetime, even right now on the spot. You don't have to wait eons and eons.

It feels that we are living in an intense time when there is so much confusion as well as so much potential. I believe that many people are ready to wake up. There is a hunger for inner freedom that comes when one sees that the wheel of delusion, confusion, and neurosis is exhausting. Luckily many people in the world have the opportunity as well as the circumstances required to practice a profound Dharma such as Dzogchen.

It is very joyous for me to write this book for various reasons. I have tremendous admiration for the eighteenth-century Dzogchen master Jigme Lingpa, who is a remarkable spiritual master. I am also a big fan of his writings, and I love his poetry. I think he is one of the more creative and original writers in the Tibetan tradition. My affinity for him developed at a very early age by practicing the Longchen Nyingthig *ngondro*, the preliminary practice in Jigme Lingpa's lineage. The lama who offered teachings on the Longchen Nyingthig ngondro was named Khenpo Choepel, an impeccable monk—kind and well-learned. I was quite young at that time, and I remember he gave that teaching during the summer, when the land in East Tibet was so beautiful, with wildflowers growing everywhere. Lots of insects and creatures come out in that season. It seemed like a heavenly realm. I was very curious about life, and there were so many possibilities in front of me on my path. I was very optimistic and at a stage of continuously falling in love with the Buddhist teachings.

When I was young, I chanted the liturgy of this Dzogchen hymn by Jigme Lingpa by myself and also chanted it in an assembly of other lamas, so this liturgy is part of my being now. Whatever we do at an early age makes a strong imprint on our lives. Just like food that you eat when you are young. For example, *tsampa,* the Tibetan barley flour, is not a fancy food but personally I have this craving from time to time to eat tsampa. I eat it with vegetables, butter, and chili sauce, and it's really delicious. I don't know if other people find it delicious but whatever food you grow up with stays with you. So the liturgies I chanted when I was growing up are like spiritual tsampa, and this Dzogchen prayer is one of them. Jigme Lingpa's teachings are a significant part of my life as well as my spirituality.

This *doha*, or song of realization, is regarded as one of the sacred texts in the Nyingma tradition. Usually one would not casually write a commentary on this doha unless there was a very compelling reason, because it is so sacred. Not to write a commentary on it is a way of respecting it and treating it as sacred. Yet somehow the right conditions ripened for me to even have the intention and courage to write a commentary. This text is not very simple; it captures not only the essential wisdom of Dzogchen but the entire subtle and sometimes challenging philosophical components of it. When I started working on this commentary, it felt like I was undertaking a formidable task. Yet I also believe in the Tibetan notion of *tendrel* (W. *rten 'brel*), auspicious interdependence of causes and conditions, which allowed me to write this book.

I feel extremely fortunate to have met with some amazing Dzogchen masters. Let me take this as an opportunity to express my highest gratitude to the Dzogchen masters who touched my heart, especially Lama Garwang. I am very thankful to Lama Garwang who gave me *ngotrod* (W. *ngo sprod*), pointing-out instructions. If not for him, I would perhaps not be writing this book. I felt that the *ngotrod,* pointing-out instruction, that he gave me was complete and perfect in itself, and that it was also permission to practice Dzogchen and to share it with others.

Personally, I hold His Holiness Khenpo Jigme Puntsok in the highest regard. To me, he was like Padmasambhava returning to the world. He was known for being very mindful of whatever he said. He was famous for saying things with great carefulness. He came to the West only one time. I saw a video clip of his teaching in the West. He was speaking to the Western disciples, encouraging them to practice Dzogchen. He basically said, just practice Dzogchen, that's all you need. He was saying it with such joy. In my opinion, he was indicating that this is the time when a massive number of people are ready to wake up and are able to understand the nondual teachings. That wasn't true in the past, when only a few individuals understood the nondual teachings.

So I think it is the perfect time to bring these teachings to a wider audience. I hope this book will serve that vision.

Writing this book was a learning process for me as well as extremely enjoyable. It made me happy just being immersed in the Dzogchen teachings. I am thankful to those who encouraged and inspired me to write this book. I'm thankful to all my friends who shower me with love and kindness, and provide me with the environment and conditions that allow me to do my work, such as writing. Here, let me express my gratitude to two individuals: Lama Lakshey Zangpo Rinpoche, who was the inspiration for me to write this book, and Laura Duggan, who tirelessly worked with me on this book as editor.

This is, in some sense, a book on a very serious topic. I hope that readers will find that it is helpful as well as enjoyable to read. Above all, I hope that this book will help readers understand the profound depth of Dzogchen teachings.

Anam Thubten

THE DZOGCHEN ASPIRATION PRAYER

By Jigme Lingpa

In Tibetan and English

ཨོཾ༔ ཀློང་ཆེན་སྙིང་གི་ཐིག་ལེ་ལས༔ གཞི་ལམ་འབྲས་བུའི་སྨོན་ལམ་བཞུགས༔

དཔལ་ཀུན་ཏུ་བཟང་པོ་ལ་ཕྱག་འཚལ་ལོ༔

1.
གདོད་མའི་གནས་ལུགས་རང་བཞིན་སྤྲོས་དང་བྲལ༔
ཡོད་པ་མ་ཡིན་རྒྱལ་བས་འདི་མ་གཟིགས༔
མེད་པ་མ་ཡིན་འཁོར་འདས་ཀུན་གྱི་གཞི༔
འགལ་འདུ་མ་ཡིན་བརྗོད་བྱའི་ཡུལ་ལས་འདས༔
རྫོགས་ཆེན་གཞི་ཡི་གནས་ལུགས་རྟོགས་པར་ཤོག༔

2.
ངོ་བོ་སྟོང་པས་རྟག་པའི་མཐའ་ལས་གྲོལ༔
རང་བཞིན་གསལ་བས་ཆད་པའི་མུ་དང་བྲལ༔
ཐུགས་རྗེ་འགག་མེད་སྣ་ཚོགས་སྤྲུལ་པའི་གཞི༔
གསུམ་དུ་དབྱེ་ཡང་དོན་ལ་ཐ་མི་དད༔
རྫོགས་ཆེན་གཞི་ཡི་གནས་ལུགས་རྟོགས་པར་ཤོག༔

3.
བསམ་གྱིས་མི་ཁྱབ་སྒྲོ་འདོགས་ཀུན་དང་བྲལ༔
ཡོད་དང་མེད་པའི་ཕྱོགས་འཛིན་རྣམ་པར་ཞིག༔
འདི་དོན་བརྗོད་ལ་རྒྱལ་བའི་ལྗགས་ཀྱང་རྡུགས༔
ཐོག་མཐའ་བར་མེད་གཉིང་གསལ་ཆེན་པོའི་དབྱིངས༔
རྫོགས་ཆེན་གཞི་ཡི་གནས་ལུགས་རྟོགས་པར་ཤོག༔

The Prayer of Ground, Path, & Fruition from the Heart Essence of the Great Expanse

Homage to glorious Samantabhadra!

1.

The true nature of the primordial state is intrinsically free from all conceptual elaborations.
It is not existent, because Buddha hasn't seen it.
It is not nonexistent; it is the ground of all samsara and nirvana.
It is not contradictory but is beyond words.
May I realize the true nature of the ground of Dzogchen.

2.

Because the essence is empty, it is free from eternalism.
Its nature is luminous, therefore it is free from nihilism.
Its compassion is ceaseless, the ground of myriad emanations.
Even though it is divided into three, they are not separate in actuality.
May I realize the true nature of the ground of Dzogchen.

3.

Inconceivable and free from all conceptual exaggerations,
The reference point to existent or nonexistent collapses.
Even Buddha's tongue struggles to describe this truth.
It has no beginning, no end, and no middle. It is a space of deep, profound clarity.
May I realize the true nature of the ground of Dzogchen.

4.

རང་ངོ་རྣམ་དག་སྐྱེ་མེད་ཀ་དག་ལ༔
ལྷུན་གྲུབ་འདུས་མ་བྱས་པའི་གདངས་ཤར་བ༔
གུད་དུ་མ་བཟུང་རིག་སྟོང་ཟུང་འཇུག་ཆེར༔
རྟོགས་པས་གཞི་ཡི་དགོངས་པ་ཚད་དུ་ཕྱིན༔
ལམ་གྱི་གནད་ལ་གོལ་འཆུགས་མེད་པར་ཤོག༔

5.

ཡེ་ནས་དག་པས་ལྟ་བའི་མིང་ཡང་མེད༔
རང་ངོ་རིག་པས་སྒོམ་རྒྱུའི་ཤུབས་ནས་འདོན༔
གཟའ་གཏད་མེད་པས་སྤྱོད་པའི་སྒྲོག་དང་བྲལ༔
རང་བཞིན་ལྷུམས་ཞུགས་སྤྲོས་བྲལ་རྗེན་པའི་ངང༔
ལམ་གྱི་གནད་ལ་གོལ་འཆུགས་མེད་པར་ཤོག༔

6.

བཟང་ངན་རྣམ་རྟོག་ཕྱོགས་སུ་མ་ལྷུང་ཞིང༔
བཏང་སྙོམས་ལུང་མ་བསྟན་དུ་མ་འབྱམས་པར༔
ཤར་གྲོལ་རིས་མེད་རྒྱ་ཡན་ལྷུན་འབྱམས་ཀློང༔
སྤང་བླང་ཡེ་ཟད་རང་བཞིན་ཡོངས་ཤེས་ངང༔
ལམ་གྱི་གནད་ལ་གོལ་འཆུགས་མེད་པར་ཤོག༔

4.
In the unborn, original purity, which is pristine in itself,
The radiance of the spontaneously present unconditioned shines,
Yet not held as something other, the great union of awareness and emptiness.
The understanding of primordial ground culminates through this realization.
May there be no pitfalls concerning the vital points of the path.

5.
From the beginning, it is already pure, and the term "view" does not even exist.
By awareness realizing its own nature, it pulls itself from the sheath of meditation.
Because there are no reference points, it is freed from the chains of conduct.
In the womb of the unconditioned nature, naked and free from conceptual elaborations,
May there be no pitfalls concerning the vital points of the path.

6.
Not falling into the partiality of good and bad thoughts
And not wandering in an undifferentiated state,
Within the limitless vast expanse, whatever arises is liberated.
By understanding the nature of reality in which all accepting and rejecting are intrinsically exhausted,
May there be no pitfalls concerning the vital points of the path.

7.
ཐོག་མའི་སྤྱི་གཞི་ནམ་མཁའ་ལྟ་བུའི་ངང༔
གཞི་སྣང་རིག་པ་མཁའ་ལ་སྤྲིན་དེངས་བཞིན༔
ཕྱི་གསལ་ཤེས་པ་ནང་དུ་ལྡོག་པ་ལས༔
ཁྱད་ཆོས་དྲུག་ལྡན་གཞོན་ནུ་བུམ་སྐུའི་སྐྱབས༔
འབྲས་བུའི་རྒྱལ་པོ་བཙན་ས་ཟིན་པར་ཤོག༔

8.
ཡེ་ནས་རང་རིག་ཀུན་ཏུ་བཟང་པོ་ལ༔
ཐོབ་བྱའི་ཞེ་འདོད་མཐའ་དག་དབྱིངས་སུ་ཡལ༔
བྱ་རྩོལ་བློ་འདས་རྫོགས་པ་ཆེན་པོའི་གཤིས༔
དབྱིངས་རིག་ཀུན་ཏུ་བཟང་མོའི་མཁའ་ཀློང་སྐྱབས༔
འབྲས་བུའི་རྒྱལ་པོ་བཙན་ས་ཟིན་པར་ཤོག༔

9.
རབ་ཏུ་མི་གནས་དབུ་མ་ཆེན་པོའི་དོན༔
ཁྱབ་གདལ་ལྷུན་འབྱམས་ཕྱག་རྒྱ་ཆེན་པོའི་ངང༔
མཐའ་གྲོལ་ཀློང་ཡངས་རྫོགས་པ་ཆེན་པོའི་གནད༔
ས་ལམ་ཡོན་ཏན་གཞིར་རྫོགས་ལྷུན་གྲུབ་སྐྱབས༔
འབྲས་བུའི་རྒྱལ་པོ་བཙན་ས་ཟིན་པར་ཤོག༔

7.
Within the space-like original primordial ground,
Just like clouds dissolve into the sky, the display of ground-
awareness dissolves.
The outwardly illuminated mind reverses and goes inward.
Within the state of the youthful vase body endowed with
the six qualities,
May I reach the citadel of the king of all fruitions.

8.
To Samantabhadra, the primordial self-aware awareness,
All the notions of attainment dissolve into space.
The nature of Ati Yoga goes beyond effort and mind.
In the expansive womb of Samantabhadri, the union of
space and awareness,
May I reach the citadel of the king of all fruitions.

9.
The meaning of the Great Middle Way—non-abiding.
The nature of Mahamudra—all-encompassing and
spontaneously pervasive.
The vital point of Dzogchen—liberation from extremes
and expansive.
The qualities of the bhumis and path are complete within
ground—within the spontaneously present state.
May I reach the citadel of the king of all fruitions.

ཐུགས་བཅུད་ཀློང་ཆེན་ཟབ་རྒྱ་ཡིཿ
མཐའ་སྤུད་སྨོན་ལམ་ཟབ་མོ་འདིཿ
བཀའ་སྲུང་དྲང་སྲོང་རཱ་ཧུ་ལཿ
བརྩེའི་ཚུལ་གྱིས་བསྐུལ་ནས་བཀོདཿ
ཟབ་དོན་སྤེལ་བ་དོན་ཡོད་ཅིངཿ
རྟེན་འབྲེལ་སྨོན་ལམ་མཐར་ཕྱིན་ཕྱིརཿ
ནམ་མཁའི་སྙིང་པོས་བྱིན་རླབས་པའིཿ
ཀོང་སྨྱོན་སྨྲས་པའི་རིག་འཛིན་ལཿ
ཟབ་རྒྱ་བཀྲོལ་ཏེ་གཏད་རྒྱ་བྲུསཿ
འགྲོ་དོན་ནམ་མཁའ་མཉམ་པར་ཤོགཿ

Colophon:

The quintessence of enlightened mind, the profound seal of the great expanse,
concludes with this profound aspiration prayer.
The guardian of the teachings, the sage Rahula,
appeared in the form of a monk, and at his request, it was composed.
In order to benefit others by spreading its profound meaning,
and to complete the auspicious interdependence and aspirations,
to the one who was blessed by Namkhi Nyingpo,
the hidden Vidyadhara, the crazy one from Kong-po,
I opened this profound seal and entrusted him with it.
May its benefit for others become as vast as space.

The Tradition of Dzogchen

Most spiritual traditions have two dimensions. One is exoteric, which can be communicated easily to most people. Another dimension is esoteric, which often appears to be obscure and only a few understand it. This is true for Buddhism. But then there is Dzogchen, which cannot easily be put into either of these categories. On the one hand, its truth cannot be easily understood by most people. It requires a special mind or level of spiritual development for someone to really understand it. And yet it is not esoteric, because the truth it expresses is both profound and simple. It is not shrouded in the trappings of magical rituals and abstract theories.

Dzogchen itself is not an "ism" and cannot be defined in the realm of a particular tradition or culture. At the same time, entire sets of teachings as well as lineages are dedicated to illuminating its truths to the world. Other traditions also illuminate these truths, which are timeless and universal. One should always be cautious not to define them. One of the safest words to denote the truth of Dzogchen is ineffable.

Dzogchen is a system that emphasizes the direct awakening to nature of mind, or *rigpa* (W. *rig pa*). It is not any kind of creed or some particular doctrine that we can hold onto or define. Rigpa, or awareness, is the most important theme in all of Dzogchen. Rigpa is described as the unconditioned, the buddha mind, or the highest state of awakening. Yet it is not like some kind of supreme, transcendent consciousness that is distant from us. Instead, it can be so simple that an individual can experience it at any given moment. And when one experiences rigpa, it often doesn't come as some kind of grand vision or experience; it can be shockingly simple. Later in this book, we will explore what rigpa is. One of the hindrances to awakening to rigpa is our tendency to mystify it, therefore Dzogchen masters often take a lot of time demystifying rigpa.

So we can say that Dzogchen is a particular practice that has its own history and tradition while it illuminates a timeless, universal truth. It can be regarded as the nondual aspect of Buddhism that transcends most doctrines.

When we human beings become religious, almost automatically we seek a doctrine that we can rely on and use as a guide, as a sacred compass to navigate the realm of this life and its complexity. We use it to find the demarcation between good and bad, ethical guidelines, and answers to the unknown. Doctrines often come with quite detailed concepts and theories as well as a whole set of observances. All this could have the power to make us better people. At the same time, this does have limitations, and at some point, these trappings become a hindrance to the highest transcendence, the total liberation that we long for.

There are individuals throughout history who came to a crossroad in their spiritual journey where they wanted to outgrow all the conceptual doctrines, rules, and regulations—the nitty-gritty religious observances—and wanted to experience absolute freedom. They wanted a state where they were no longer bound by the chains of the mundane world and were freed from the chains of dualistic doctrines.

Many individuals who call themselves spiritual or religious feel that they have been on a journey of awakening or inner transformation. Yet at some point, they feel exhausted on their journey, especially if the journey feels too arduous or futile, and the destination is not in sight. They may have a sense that the journey itself has become the very realm from which they want to be free. They want to drop the inner burdens completely, to drop anything that binds them, and to experience the highest freedom, a freedom that was tasted by all the great beings, such as Buddha. They might want to experience the profound awakening that Siddhartha experienced under the bodhi tree.

At some point on the path, a powerful impulse arises in some individuals for a shortcut, for a more radical approach that takes one to the heart of the matter. Yet this impulse is quite courageous, a kind of divine *chutzpah*. It is chutzpah because people have a fear of making the radical jump into absolute freedom. There were many people who felt they were not good enough, not ready to practice Dzogchen, because it requires a kind of divine chutzpah to drop all the struggles on the spiritual journey and experience the highest freedom here and now. Dzogchen was even shunned, and many opponents in the past wrote texts refuting it. For these reasons, Dzogchen was kept secret, and the ancient masters taught it in a more quiet fashion, often to select individuals who were ready or courageous enough to practice it.

Originally, Dzogchen was taught in India by masters such as Prahevajra, Manjushrimitra, and Shri Singha. Then in the eighth century, it was brought to Tibet from India by

Padmasambhava and Vimalamitra. At Samye Monastery, which was the first Buddhist monastery in Tibet, the Tibetan translator Vairotsana translated numerous Dzogchen texts, especially the Dzogchen Tantras, from Sanskrit. At that time, many monastics as well as lay people, including the king himself, practiced Dzogchen. It became a lineage that continues even today.

The tradition of Dzogchen went through ups and downs throughout history. Sometimes it was kept more secret, and at other times it had a relatively great following and popularity. It is mainly taught in the Nyingma lineage, which became the guardian of the Dzogchen lineage, whereas other traditions in Tibet have their own version of nondual teachings, such as Mahamudra.

Dzogchen is an abbreviation of the Tibetan term, *dzog pa chen po* (W. *rdzogs pa chen po*), the Great Completion. The meaning of the word *Dzogchen* is not static and can be described in many ways. The term could be split into two parts, *dzog pa* and *chen po*. *Dzog pa* means completion, which denotes that all phenomena of the outer world as well as the mental world, the entire existence that we perceive, samsara and nirvana, are completely contained within the realm of nature of mind, *sem nyi* (W. *sems nyid*), pure awareness, or rigpa. It means that everything is a pure display of rigpa. Nothing is separate from it. *Chen po,* or great, has a similar meaning; that is, this truth encompasses everything, and nothing is excluded from the truth. *Great* also means that this is the highest truth that there is.

Today, nature of mind and the teachings of Dzogchen are becoming more known among meditators. Nature of mind is defined with poetic and intuitive language because it is your individual, subjective experience that has no particular characteristics, no color or shape. If you are describing your laptop or computer, you can spend a lot of time describing the size, length, color, material, and so forth. You can even describe your thoughts or emotions with quite precise and logical language. Whereas the nature of mind doesn't have any particular characteristics. We can be very specific about anger or worry. But the nature of mind is more intuitive and subtle. Therefore Dzogchen uses poetic expressions, like luminous, spacious, limitless. Those descriptions of the nature of mind are often voiced by many of the great yogis who experienced the nature of mind and resided there most of the time. Yogis such as Shabkar and Milarepa spent a lot of time in the mountains dwelling in a state of mind that is spacious, limitless, not contracted, filled with peace, serenity, and joy. Sometimes the nature of mind is accompanied by intuitive insight, understanding the bigger picture of reality such as the nature of all things. In their dohas, these yogis invite us to taste and glimpse the nature of mind.

Ati Yoga

Dzogchen is also known in Sanskrit as *Ati Yoga*, or *Mahasandhi*, which is the highest *yana*. Mahayana Buddhism uses a framework known as the yanas to describe the stages of individual spiritual growth as well as the hierarchy of spiritual awakening and the path. Indeed, there is a hierarchy in the realm of spirituality, just as in anything else. Some levels of spiritual development are more profound, more advanced than others. This is not about comparing oneself to others; it can be seen even in one's own spiritual journey. If someone looks back, she or he will realize that their current spiritual development is much more advanced than perhaps ten years ago. She or he will see there are fewer burdens in their consciousness and more wisdom.

Mahayana Buddhism has numerous ways of laying out this framework. There could be two yanas, or three yanas. The Nyingma tradition lays out nine yanas, which is unique to its system and does not exist in other Mahayana traditions. The nine yanas are a wonderful system that addresses the subtleties in the hierarchy of spiritual development. We will discuss the nine yanas in more detail in a later chapter.

Dzogchen is the last of the nine yanas and is called Ati Yoga or the highest yoga, the unsurpassable yoga. All the other yanas except Dzogchen are in some way based on the notion that one has to exert effort or have some kind of strategy to reach enlightenment. The other yanas also have some limiting theories. Therefore, Dzogchen refers to itself as "the yana beyond mind," which indicates that all the other paths are in the realm of the conceptual or dualistic mind that still holds onto duality: there is "me," the seeker; enlightenment is over there; there is the path that "I" am going to travel; and "I" will go through karmic purification using various means to reach enlightenment. Paths other than Dzogchen often try to capture the ultimate truth in logic, theories, and concepts, yet the ultimate transcends everything. The ultimate truth can never be fully captured in words and concepts.

Dzogchen transcends all the doctrines, spiritual practices, and disciplines. This does not mean that Dzogchen practitioners do not observe the practices of the other yanas. Many monks and nuns faithfully observe monastic disciplines yet may also practice Dzogchen. Similarly there are tantrikas who observe the Vajrayana disciplines and are immersed in sadhanas while still practicing Dzogchen. So the individual doesn't have to drop any of the other paths, even though Dzogchen itself goes beyond all of them. Some individuals mainly focus on the practice of Dzogchen and leave all the other disciplines behind.

Three Auspicious Conditions for Awakening

Dzogchen also emphasizes the notion of radical awakening, which is like a powerful epiphany in which one can make a huge leap from one level of spiritual development to a higher level of inner awakening without going through the usual process. It is so powerful that many of our karmic tendencies, which otherwise would take years of hard work for karmic purification, can be purified in such a moment. Not only that, it can happen almost spontaneously, unlike an insight that is a product of accumulating knowledge, doing spiritual practices, and which comes into being in a linear fashion.

When one meets with the right master, right circumstances, and right state of mind, such radical awakening can happen. When the three auspicious conditions come together, such awakening is possible for anyone. The three conditions are meeting with an awakened master, a lineage with a blessing, and a disciple with devotion. It is like having the ideal conditions. Imagine that such awakening is like a beautiful flower. With the right temperature, soil, water, and so on, the flower can blossom.

Awakened Master

The awakened master is someone who does not just have intellectual understanding of the absolute truth but who has realized it experientially, so much so that he or she lives that realization. There is so much emphasis on the need for finding the right master in the Buddhist tradition that many meditators in the past undertook entire quests to find the right master. Somebody might have ample knowledge about Dzogchen texts and tantras, but he or she may not have the direct experience of the absolute truth. Then that person would not be considered an awakened master.

This is not just an old theory. This idea still holds truth. There are many accounts where people studied Dzogchen texts and they still couldn't have the direct experience of it. Then finally they met with somebody who was able to help them to have the direct realization of the absolute truth, which is the buddha mind.

It is not really easy to find out who is an awakened master and who is not. This is a difficult area. Someone could be very famous, or speak very well about Dzogchen teachings, or may look like a Dzogchen master who fulfills our wild fantasies about being carefree and so forth, but this could just be a performance. So it is very difficult to know who is awakened. One needs to have a higher, intuitive intelligence to discern the character of someone else. Sometimes you will know afterwards if someone helped you to wake up.

Lineage with Blessing

The second auspicious condition is the lineage with a blessing. Blessing here is the potency to awaken our consciousness. The blessing of the lineage is that such a lineage is authentic, has been blessed by true masters from the past, and sometimes also has a sacred track record of producing awakened yogis and yoginis. In the Nyingma tradition, you don't just study Dzogchen with anyone unless you are sure about the lineage. For example, the practitioners of Dzogchen are encouraged to remember the entire history of the lineage.

The two most important Dzogchen masters in Tibet are Padmasambhava, who brought Vajrayana and Dzogchen to Tibet, and Yeshe Tsogyal, who at one time was the queen of Tibet. Later she renounced mundane life and became a yogini. She also taught Dzogchen. Their lineage is the living spirit of the Nyingma tradition even today. In Tibet, all the Dzogchen lineages are one way or another connected to these two masters.

Perhaps one of the most authentic and powerful lineages in Tibetan Buddhism is the Longchen Nyingthig, which is part of the Nyingma lineage. The Longchen Nyingthig lineage has been famous for producing many awakened individuals. The lineage started in the eighteenth century with Jigme Lingpa, who was a prolific writer, poet, and visionary. He had a powerful awakening, which he attributed to the blessings of Longchenpa, who can easily be regarded as one of the most important Dzogchen masters in the entire history of Tibet. Then Jigme Lingpa gave Dzogchen transmission to many disciples, many of whom became awakened, and his lineage began to spread throughout Tibet and beyond.

Jigme Lingpa's two main disciples who continued his lineage were Drodupchen Jigme Trinley Ozer and Jigme Gyalwe Nyugu, whose disciple was Patrul Rinpoche, the great Dzogchen master of the nineteenth century. Patrul Rinpoche's disciple was Nyoshul Lungtok Tenpa Nyima, whose disciple was Khenpo Ngagi Wangpo, whose disciples became the most important Dzogchen masters in the twentieth century. Today many people in Tibet who practice Dzogchen trace their lineage to the Longchen Nyingthig masters.

Another well-known master is Shabkar, who was also trained in the Longchen Nyingthig lineage. He wrote a well-known text called *The Flight of the Garuda*, which is one of the clearest books about Dzogchen. It has been translated into different languages, and many Western Dharma practitioners told me that it is their favorite Dzogchen text.

Devotion

The third auspicious condition is a disciple with devotion. Here, having devotion should be defined very carefully; otherwise, one could have all kinds of wild and mistaken notions about what it might be. It is more than being someone who has spiritual zeal. It refers to someone whose heart is very wide open and is willing to drop the ego defenses, someone who has the ability to surrender the ego to the absolute truth, to freedom. It is someone who has true humility and also has a longing to wake up at any cost. It is someone who is very determined. One doesn't have to demonstrate it in some outward behavior. Many anecdotes from the past remind us of the importance of devotion. Without such devotion, even if Prahevajra himself or Yeshe Tsogyal knocked on your door, nothing would happen. It would be like pouring water on a rock—nothing would grow.

The opposite of devotion in this context is resistance, which could take all kinds of forms. Some of them are tricky, deceptive, and hard to detect. Some are obvious, like someone lost in his or her ego who doesn't want to change, or wants to live unconsciously, glorify the ego, and indulge in hatred and greed. But there are more subtle forms of resistance. Someone might appear very spiritual, actively looking for awakening and the wisdom of Dzogchen but may have resistance instead of an open heart, or wants to indulge in theories and concepts rather than wake up. Therefore resistance can take many forms.

Devotion is like an antidote to clear away all the resistance. Devotion is something we can develop. Don't worry if you don't have devotion. It is not an inborn phenomenon that you have or don't have. It can be cultivated just like anything else. This is why there are preliminary practices in the Nyingma tradition that are quite lengthy. Many of them are designed as a system or process where the student can cultivate such devotion. In that sense, devotion is perhaps the most important criterion of a student who is capable of radical awakening.

Spontaneous Awakening

There are inspiring anecdotes where people had a spontaneous awakening through a variety of catalysts. I heard a somewhat humorous story about a lama in the Kham region of Tibet who was offering Dzogchen teachings. Most of the disciples felt that they had realized awareness, buddha mind, rigpa. But there was one student who didn't get it, no matter how much his master tried to point it out to him. He didn't give up, because he was sincere and full of devotion. One day, the lama said, "Pick up a bag of barley from my house and run to the top of the mountain without looking back or taking a break." The student was so respectful to his master that he was willing to do this. No doubt he was very intelligent, so he knew his master was trustworthy. He didn't have blind faith. He listened to his master's advice, even though it was totally weird. He picked up a bag of barley from his master's house and started running at the fastest speed. At one point running up the mountain, he lost his breath and fell down, totally exhausted. All his thoughts of past, present, and future, all reference points, every notion of reality completely dissolved. In that moment, there were no more concepts, and he realized what his teacher was trying to tell him. He had a direct experience of rigpa. He was so happy he wanted to report it to his master, and with childlike joy, he started running to his teacher's house with the greatest speed. He finally got back to his master's house and shouted, "Now I saw it. I realized it." The master said, "I don't care if you are awakened or not. Where is my bag of barley?"

Another famous anecdote about spontaneous awakening concerns the renowned eighth-century Dzogchen master and translator Vairotsana. Once he was slandered by others, and people made up stories about him, forcing the Tibetan King Trisong Detsen to exile Vairotsana to Tsawa Rong (Gyarong) in eastern Tibet. Eventually Vairotsana was allowed to return to central Tibet. On the way back, a very old man met with Vairotsana and asked him, "Where are you from, and where are you going?"

Vairotsana replied that he came from Gyarong and was going to central Tibet. The old man said, with a disbelieving expression, "That's unbelievable. Why don't you stay in Gyarong and study with the master Vairotsana. You must be deluded."

Vairotsana said, "Vairotsana? That's me!"

At that moment, this man was so happy and joyous that he hugged Vairotsana and cried for a while. He said, "I'm old. Give me the teachings that will benefit me at the time of death."

Vairotsana accepted his request. Most probably, this old man would not have understood a scholarly lecture. So instead, Vairotsana did something quite improvisational: he put his meditation sash around the old man's body and invited him to sit. That simple act by Vairotsana became a pith instruction, or *dam ngak* (W. *gdams ngag*), and in that moment, the old man spontaneously awakened to the nature of his own mind. This old man is a very important figure in the Dzogchen lineage. His name is Pham Mipham Gonpo.

So there are countless such anecdotes of spontaneous awakening where the three auspicious circumstances—an awakened master, a lineage with blessing, and devotion—came together.

Pointing-Out Instruction

Spontaneous awakening often happens during *ngotrod* (W. *ngo sprod*), which is the pointing-out instruction. A pointing-out instruction often can be an improvisational teaching, not like a usual teaching where somebody gives a formal sermon on a body of knowledge. It can be very improvisational, like Vairotsana was with Pham Mipham Gonpo. You never know how the master is going to give that teaching. They don't open some text and give a philosophical commentary. Sometimes the master might speak a lot and sometimes only give a few words. Sometimes the teaching could be delivered through gestures, or energetic movement, or body language. Yet when there is the right moment, often the student can directly experience rigpa, or nature of mind, which is the non-egoic state of consciousness.

Jigme Lingpa

Jigme Lingpa is a very important individual in the Dzogchen lineage because he revived the potency of the Dzogchen practice in Tibet. Throughout history, there were times when it was taught with a liberating potency, then it might have gone into hiding for a while, then again a master would come who revived its power to liberate, and many people would wake up. Jigme Lingpa is one of the people who brought back the potency. Some say that the reason Dzogchen is widely practiced now is because of him. Even today, most of the Dzogchen masters trace their lineage back to Jigme Lingpa at some point.

Jigme Lingpa was an extraordinarily erudite and prolific writer. He wrote many important texts on Buddhist doctrine, and he was also a poet, who had great originality in his writings. He was so respected and loved that high lamas of every Buddhist tradition studied with him. That was unusual since often lamas didn't study and take teachings from those outside their own tradition. At the time when he lived, Gelug was the dominant tradition and was governing Tibet, yet some of the most eminent Gelugpa lamas followed his teachings. He spent a lot of time—years and years—practicing meditation in solitude. After he had a series of powerful epiphanies, he founded the Longchen Nyingthig. He wrote his autobiography, which clearly explains his own journey as well as the epiphanies he went through.

Dzogchen Aspiration Prayer

There are numerous Dzogchen texts, such as the *Seventeen Dzogchen Tantras*. Longchenpa himself wrote volumes of texts on Dzogchen. Many of them are quite extensive and deal not only with the meditative practice of Dzogchen but also with the philosophy of Dzogchen, which is vast and expansive. Dzogchen has a rich philosophy that describes the ultimate truth, how our mind constructs reality, different stages of awakening, attributes of enlightenment, and so on. Yet many of the Dzogchen texts can take a lengthy time and a lot of study to really go through them. There are individuals who spend a great deal of time learning and perfecting their knowledge of these treatises. On the other hand, without learning the complexities of this philosophical system, one can be awakened simply by realizing the heart of the matter.

The text by Jigme Lingpa that we are going to review in this book is a *monlam*, or aspiration prayer, which is a genre of Tibetan literature. There are numerous aspiration prayers. Some are from the sutras, and some of them are from Vajrayana. This text is considered the Dzogchen aspiration prayer. Even though it is quite short, it captures the entirety of the Dzogchen teachings. This prayer is so loved that even today in the monasteries the monks and nuns chant this liturgy with the aspiration to be awakened. They also chant it when someone has died.

This can be a perfect liturgy to chant every day if someone wants to practice Dzogchen. Some individuals in Tibet chant Dzogchen liturgies to align their mind with the liberating wisdom of Dzogchen, but some of these liturgies are very long. This aspiration prayer is perfect—it is profound and also convenient to chant as a daily practice.

This precious text by Jigme Lingpa should not be regarded as just another writing but as a *terma* (W. *gter ma*), a treasure revelation that is an expression of the dharmakaya mind, or enlightened mind. One can read and recite this text in order to understand Dzogchen, and it can also be used for daily meditation guidance as a way to connect with the lineage of Dzogchen.

The Title

The Prayer of Ground, Path & Fruition
From the Heart Essence of the Great Expanse

The title is considered the window through which the entire body of a teaching can be seen. There is even a theory in the Buddhist tradition that someone who is extremely intelligent can understand the entire content of a text by simply looking at the title. Therefore, the early writers paid great attention to the title of the book they were about to write. Not only that, whenever a master gives an oral commentary on any classical text, she or he will sometimes expound a lengthy commentary on the title that could go on for hours and hours. Sometimes the title of a Tibetan text can be quite long and can give you a sense of the text's contents.

Here, the title of this text begins by denoting the tradition that this prayer belongs to, which is the Longchen Nyingthig lineage founded by Jigme Lingpa. The translation of Longchen Nyingthig is "heart essence of the great expanse." The term *great expanse* can have many meanings. It can refer to the notion of the great, limitless, enlightened mind, which can be compared to an inexhaustible treasure of wisdom that abruptly poured out from the consciousness of Jigme Lingpa and was revealed in the profound teachings that he wrote.

This means that many of his writings are not considered ordinary writings or written from his own intellect. Instead, he tapped into an intellect beyond mind, where timeless wisdom flows. Often, masters like Jigme Lingpa composed many of these teachings spontaneously; traditionally, the master dictated, and some disciple would write them down. The master didn't have to struggle or think about what to say. It was as if the master was reading a text rather than writing. In the Nyingma tradition, these texts are called *termas* or treasures, revelatory writings.

Nyingthig, or heart essence, is a term that is used quite often in the Nyingma writings and particularly in the revelatory writings or terma. It means the text is the distilled essence or quintessence of an entire cycle of teachings. *Heart essence* also means that the teaching is truly profound and utterly cherished by the masters of the lineage.

Genre

The title says it is "the aspiration prayer of ground, path, and fruition." This is the genre of the text: an aspiration prayer. It is an aspiration to become enlightened by realizing the profound wisdom of Dzogchen and reaching the highest awakening, the nondual awakening. One can easily see that this is the highest form of aspiration prayer when it is compared with the many other aspiration prayers that exist in the Mahayana tradition.

This text is more than an aspiration prayer. It is also a *doha*, a song of realization. It is poetic and has verses that perfectly express the entirety of Dzogchen as an independent and complete tradition in itself.

Framework: Ground, Path, Fruition

According to Tibetan Buddhist masters, every tradition in Buddhism has its own complete system comprised of the three principles of ground, path, and fruition, or *zhi, lam, and dri (W: gzhi, lam, 'bras)*. In simple terms, ground is where we start from, the fruition is where we want to go, and the path is how to get there.

This turns out to be an excellent framework that can completely describe an entire tradition. If one of the three principles is missing, then the framework of that tradition would be incomplete. Imagine that a tradition is like a building. If the foundation or windows or doors or roof are not there, then the architecture is not complete. That's the relationship between a tradition and this framework. According to the Tibetan masters or *panditas*, scholars, all the Buddhist traditions have these three principles.

This is also a useful way to understand the uniqueness of a tradition. However, between Buddhist traditions, those three principles can contrast with each other quite a lot. Sometimes one wonders whether the traditions come from the same root or not, except for fundamental principles that bring them together, like the doctrine of no-self or the practice of nonviolence. Other than that, the contrast between the principles is so big that even the concept of enlightenment could be defined in such a way that some traditions could discredit or debunk another tradition's version of enlightenment as incomplete or pseudo-nirvana.

As we go through the commentary, it will be useful to go through the three principles of ground, path, and fruition of Dzogchen and also refer to the principles of other traditions, not to put them down but to see the contrast. Often the three principles in other traditions appear more dualistic when they are compared with those of Dzogchen.

Homage

Homage to glorious Samantabhadra!

Paying homage to a buddha or lineage master is a standard way of beginning a text in the Buddhist tradition. It is not paying homage just to a noble figure but to someone who is related to the lineage or the text that one is about to write.

Here, the author is paying homage to Buddha Samantabhadra, who is the primordial Buddha in the Dzogchen Tantras. The very root of the Dzogchen lineage is traced back to Samantabhadra, who is not an individual. Samantabhadra is the source of the Dzogchen lineage and is loved and worshipped by Dzogchen yogis.

The notion of the primordial Buddha exists in various tantras but in Dzogchen, the primordial Buddha Samantabhadra is considered the first Buddha that ever existed. However, Samantabhadra should not be defined as an individual existing within a time period. Saying *first* often gives an idea of time, and we automatically think there is literally an individual who became enlightened. Such a misconception is understandable, because we associate buddhas with an individual like Shakyamuni Buddha, who was born in India, embarked on a spiritual journey, and became awakened. So it is easy for us to anthropomorphize

Samantabhadra, but that would be an erroneous understanding. Buddha Samantabhadra cannot be defined as a particular person who was born in a certain time and place, and who had a life story. It is not like there is a particular time long ago when such an individual became enlightened. The whole notion of time has to be removed in order to truly know what Buddha Samantabhadra is.

Buddha Samantabhadra is awakening itself, the highest awakening. There is nirvana, or awakening, otherwise no one would have been awakened. So Buddha Samantabhadra represents the existence as well as the possibility of the highest inner awakening. Sometimes Buddha Samantabhadra is expressed in iconography, because our human mind needs forms in order to pay attention or develop devotion to something. Since it is not an entity, Buddha Samantabhadra is impossible to capture in forms and symbols, yet a form can help us develop love and longing for such profound awakening.

The term *awakening* will be talked about quite a lot in this book, but awakening does not have only one definition. It has to be interpreted in context. Obviously it is not biological awakening, like awakening from sleep. Many spiritual seekers have either a precise or vague idea of what it is. It could refer to all sorts of inner epiphanies. It could refer to someone having an extramundane or transcendent spiritual experience that has a profound impact on that person's life. It could refer to awakening from delusion to wisdom, from suffering to freedom. Or it can be awakening to something very profound, like great emptiness, no-self, or dharmakaya mind. Or it can sometimes be a synonym for enlightenment or nirvana.

In the Dzogchen Tantras, when they describe Buddha Samantabhadra, they say that Buddha Samantabhadra never performed any spiritual practice, not even a speck of it. They say Buddha Samantabhadra never meditated, never went through karmic purification, and never carried out any wholesome conduct. This is quite radical, because in many sacred traditions, these are the activities that spiritual people perform in order to become enlightened. But it is another way of telling us that Buddha Samantabhadra is not an entity in the world but a pure expression of spiritual awakening itself that can happen to anybody. There is no time, place, or characteristic that defines the awakening. All the descriptions of Buddha Samantabhadra may sound paradoxical, but they transcend any possibility that Buddha Samantabhadra is any kind of individual or entity. The highest spiritual awakening itself is not bound to anything.

There are different ways to understand the etymology and meaning of the name of the primordial Buddha, Samantabhadra in Sanskrit, or Kuntuzangpo in Tibetan. Samantabhadra can be interpreted as "ever-excellent" or "universal excellence." When we think of it as ever-excellent, it refers to the nature of our mind that is always excellent, always perfect. When we consider it as universal excellence, it can refer to the nature of reality—suchness, the absolute truth, the great emptiness—that pervades everything that exists in the entire universe. In that case, *excellence* means bringing all beings to the excellence of utter liberation, utter goodness, or complete nirvana, through skillful means, wisdom, and love. So there is fluidity in interpreting the etymology of the name. It's not that one way is the only way or the correct way.

So here the author is paying homage and expressing his utmost reverence to Buddha Samantabhadra. Again, this is considered a nondual homage, because there is no duality between the author who is paying homage and Samantabhadra, since Samantabhadra is the true nature of all beings.

VERSE 1 - TRUE NATURE OF GROUND

The true nature of the primordial state is intrinsically free from all conceptual elaborations.
It is not existent, because Buddha hasn't seen it.
It is not nonexistent; it is the ground of all samsara and nirvana.
It is not contradictory but is beyond words.
May I realize the true nature of the ground of Dzogchen.

Even though enlightenment is not a destination, a physical place, our mind has to create a conceptual map even just to embark on the inner journey, the journey of the mind. In the beginning, our mind needs to have a picture of "me" who is the traveler. Then there is the inner path that we are traveling. And there is a destination—*nirvana*, *moksha*—that we are going to arrive at. That conceptual map is needed in the beginning, though in the end that map has to be transcended. Unless that map is transcended, it becomes another concept that reifies enlightenment, which is much bigger than our ideas of it, and which can never be fully expressed in words and concepts. Even the very notion of enlightenment that we desire is just another concept from the point of view of the ultimate truth. But we need the conceptual map no matter how limited it is in itself. It helps us to move forward and inspires us to engage with the necessary means to find inner liberation.

Because Dzogchen is profoundly simple and transcends all philosophical trappings, many men and women became enlightened right on the spot through Dzogchen. They realized the very heart of Dzogchen without needing to study and memorize all the philosophical, doctrinal complexities. Yet Dzogchen is also a very rich tradition that lies on a solid ground of history, lineage, and an entire philosophical system. Getting to know its philosophical system can help us understand the nature of reality, who we are, how samsara comes into being, and what nirvana is. Such understanding can help us not only to have a rich knowledge of these points but can bring about inner liberation through a powerful awakening.

Similarly, this doha of Dzogchen is both poetic and simple, and at the same time, it lays out the entire framework of Dzogchen philosophy, which is based on ground, path, and fruition. There are, no doubt, individuals who became enlightened by practicing the Dzogchen tradition without having a very refined philosophical knowledge of those three principles. That is possible. Yet it would be very meaningful for those who are interested in Dzogchen to know the three principles. Without knowing the three principles of ground, path, and fruition, one would not have a complete picture of Dzogchen as a tradition.

Ground: Zhi

As we noted, ground, or zhi, is one of the three principles, along with path and fruition, that Tibetan Buddhist scholars often use as a framework to lay out the entire body of a tenet, philosophical system, or even a whole tradition. In that general context, the ground can be regarded as the pivotal principle upon which the entire framework of a system exists. Without it, the whole system cannot be established. Within Sutrayana, sometimes the ground might be a system of aggregates, such as the *dhatus*, faculties, and so forth. Sometimes in Sutrayana and Vajrayana, buddha nature might be regarded as the ground.

In Dzogchen, there are a few ways we can talk about ground. We could regard ground as the primordially residing rigpa that is in each of us. It could also be considered the very nature of all things. It can also be called primordial ground, or *ye zhi* (W. *ye gzhi*), which is ineffable, beyond words and concepts. Primordial ground is the state of consciousness prior to ego. It is like the *dharmadhatu*, in which everything arises and into which everything dissolves. There are different ways to talk about ground in Dzogchen, but they are the same in essence.

In this verse, the notion of ground is referring to an ineffable state of reality from which everything arises: consciousness, delusion, and freedom. It would be difficult to comprehend the teachings of Dzogchen unless this notion of ground is fully captured.

The traditional texts begin by pointing out the pseudo or flawed ground, in order to make sure that zhi is not misunderstood. It can be misunderstood quite easily when we use our rational mind to figure it out. Such misunderstandings happened quite often in the past, so the classical texts lay out the list of false zhi to make sure that we won't hold onto the wrong zhi. That whole conversation can be quite scholarly, and perhaps many yogis might not dare to attempt it, because it gets very theoretical. But it is part of classical Dzogchen.

The classical texts lay out seven different definitions of zhi that are considered flawed or wrong. This is called postulating the seven faulty grounds, *zhi dün kyön chen du tenpa* (W. *gzhi bdun skyon can du bstan pa*). The seven zhi are possible mistaken beliefs that our mind can construct in an attempt to understand the ineffable. Here is an analogy for why the correct understanding of ground is so important: Imagine you are driving somewhere, and you come to an intersection. No matter how fast your car can go, if you take the wrong turn, you will get lost. In the same way, if you misunderstand zhi, then the whole Dzogchen system is really messed up. Therefore, it is quite important to have an accurate understanding of zhi.

The texts encourage us to get rid of all the imperfect, incomplete, misconstrued notions of zhi, in order to make space for the true understanding of zhi to arise. If one wants to learn about the flawed zhi, one might have to study other texts, especially the works of Longchenpa. The main point is to get rid of all the rigid theories we might have about zhi, because the theories can often obscure the very nature of zhi, which is unconditioned and ineffable.

"The true nature of the primordial state is intrinsically free from all conceptual elaborations."

When we say *zhi*, the mind wants to point out what it is. But this verse is saying there is nothing that you can point out as zhi. There is not a single speck of anything in the entire universe that you can point to as zhi, either in physical matter or in the mental dimension. So zhi cannot be defined. Zhi itself is ineffable. It is beyond ordinary intellect and beyond the domain of words and concepts, so this verse is pointing out what zhi is not. It is using the standard Mahayana Buddhist way of defining the ineffable as that which is free from what are called the eight conceptual elaborations.

What are the eight conceptual elaborations? In the traditional texts, they are: arising, ceasing, existing, not existing, coming, going, being multiple, and being single. These elaborations don't exist in the ultimate truth. They are just part of the thinking mind, even though they seem to be so real. We use these eight conceptual elaborations to define all of reality, yet they are purely mental constructs. By setting zhi free from the two conceptual elaborations of existent and nonexistent, the verse is showing that zhi is also beyond the rest of the eight conceptual elaborations.

"It is not existent, because Buddha hasn't seen it."

Zhi is beyond the matrix of the thinking mind. In our mind, things are either existent or nonexistent. But the verse is saying zhi is neither one. This can confuse our usual thinking mind, so the verse presents reasoning to show why ground is neither existent nor nonexistent. We could call this nondual reasoning as it is not our usual logic. Our human mind wants to put everything in conceptual pigeonholes, which makes sense in everyday life. If something is not nonexistent, we think it should be existent. But that logic does not work when it comes to the ineffable. So the verse is using special logic to debunk the concept that zhi is existent.

The ultimate logic is that Buddha hasn't seen it. Here, Buddha doesn't refer to one Buddha but refers to someone who is not deluded, someone who sees the way things are, so his or her consciousness can be reliable. Whereas the minds of ordinary beings are often not reliable. So there is no "thing" that Buddha has seen as ground. The verse is using this as the highest testimony to say that ground is not existent. If it is existent, Buddha's awakened mind should have seen it. This powerful logic is used in the Buddhist tradition to negate all sorts of delusions and manufactured reality that often cast a spell on the human mind.

Not only is our thinking mind not reliable, but our five senses are not always reliable either. In general, we trust our senses. If we see something with our eyes, we think that is a valid reason to affirm existence or nonexistence of such reality. But often the Buddhist teachings say that our minds and even our senses are enchanted by delusions and cannot be relied on. So the mind of Buddha is the best testimony, because it is undeluded and awakened. If the mind of Buddha hasn't seen it, it means it is not existent. If the mind of Buddha saw it, it would be existent.

So the logic is used to say that zhi is not something we can define. It doesn't have a size or shape, and it is not even a supreme being that we can conceptualize. It is very easy for the human mind to construct concepts about things that are beyond concepts—to turn the ineffable into a concept and turn the infinite into the finite, with the best intention, sometimes in a sneaky way. When we say ground is ineffable, the mind can conjure up some thing, some entity that is big, transcendental, mighty, powerful, god-like, or some kind of energy or universal consciousness. Before you know it, the understanding of ground is tainted by eternalism and theism.

"It is not nonexistent; it is the ground of all samsara and nirvana. It is not contradictory but is beyond words."

But if something is not existent, then the mind thinks it is nonexistent, because that logic works in ordinary life. But zhi is not nonexistent either. Nonexistence is nihilism, and zhi transcends eternalism and nihilism. It is not nonexistent, because it functions as the ground from which everything arises. If it were nonexistent, it couldn't function as the source of the whole reality from which all things arise.

Usually this sounds contradictory to the logical mind. It is not contradictory—it is the way things are. It is the biggest truth, the cosmic truth that describes the mystery of everything. But that mystery is ineffable. It is not something that can be logically dissected or figured out.

When the Dzogchen Tantras talk about primordial ground, ye zhi, as the origin of samsara and nirvana, it should not be understood in the context of time. I think one miscomprehension that can happen when people read Dzogchen texts is that they think that primordial ground existed a long time ago, a really, really long time ago before the universe popped up. They think that before anything came to exist, there was this thing called primordial ground. So some people might relate to primordial ground in terms of time.

But it has nothing to do with time. Primordial ground is not something that happened in the past before we became deluded and is not here anymore. Primordial ground has no time; it transcends the three times: it has no past, it has no present, it has no future, and yet it is always here. This is quite important because when we read the Dzogchen teachings, language can be very limiting, and our mind has a tendency to interpret all these nonconceptual notions through our own dualistic view.

All these concepts are like a map of how nirvana, samsara, and the whole existence come into being. Obviously, the language in Dzogchen is quite different from the language of the sutras and the twelve links of interdependent origination, which is how general Buddhism describes how existence arises. Dzogchen's language is very poetic and uplifting as it describes how our reality comes into being. Whenever someone wants to study these things, it is important to bear in mind that one cannot be too rational or logical; otherwise, these teachings won't be approachable. The reader should remember that they have to be read from a different state of mind.

Three Kayas in Mahayana

There are important theoretical principles that serve as the backbone of almost all traditions in Mahayana, including Dzogchen, such as the three *kayas*. The three kayas appear quite often in Dzogchen teachings, and it would be difficult to understand the doctrine of Dzogchen unless we have some general idea about them. The notion of the three kayas does not exist in the Theravada Buddhist tradition, but it is one of the most important topics in Mahayana. Certain texts describe the three kayas from the point of view of the general Mahayana, such as *Abhisamayalankara*, a text that is studied as part of the main curriculum in the Tibetan Buddhist tradition. The description of the three kayas is found here and there in various other Mahayana texts as well. In the general Mahayana, the three kayas are like three "bodies" of a buddha.

Here, *body* does not mean a physical body but is more like a sacred dimension.

The first kaya is *dharmakaya,* the body of Dharma or the body of the truth. This is the enlightened nature of a buddha that goes beyond any limitations. It has no form, no shape, no size; it has no physical form at all. It is purely the enlightened state of a buddha. It is completely free from all descriptions. It has no particular characteristics or idiosyncrasies, and it is not a person. It is referring to the pure, enlightened state.

The second kaya, *sambhogakaya,* appears only to the vision of some bodhisattvas and is usually described as the body of a buddha that is manifested as a form with particular features or attributes, known as the five certainties, *ngé pa nga* (W. *nges pa lnga*): the certain body, the certain retinue, the certain place or realm, the certain teaching or Dharma, and the certain time. The certain body refers to a body that is always endowed with specific enlightened marks and signs. The certain retinue means that the buddha's disciples are bodhisattvas. The certain realm where the buddha resides is *Akanistha*, the most sublime realm of the buddhas. The certain Dharma means that the buddha only teaches Mahayana. The certain time means that the buddha will help all beings until samsara is empty.

The third kaya, *nirmanakaya,* refers to a buddha that has manifested in various forms in the physical, human world to help others find happiness and liberation.

These are the general Mahayana understandings of the three kayas.

Three Kayas in Dzogchen

In Dzogchen, even though the system of three kayas is applied, it is not about the three bodies of a buddha. Instead, it deals with the enlightened nature of our own consciousness, which is rigpa, or awareness. From that point of view, the three kayas do not really lie outside of us but are within the realm of our own awareness. In Dzogchen, the three kayas are different states of awareness. But what is awareness?

Dzogchen has the terms *awareness of ground* and *awareness of path*. They can sometimes be separate, but ultimately they can be merged into one in a yogi's meditative experience. But here I will not talk about the subtle demarcations of these two types of awareness nor other variations of awareness. Instead, I would like to talk about awareness in a more immediate fashion so that readers can relate to it.

Awareness, or rigpa, is not some sublime, altered, spiritual state of our mind. It can be revealed or pointed out at any given moment. Often Dzogchen masters say that if you just relax and don't do anything—don't meditate, don't follow your thoughts—what remains is a very alert, present awareness that is not bound by your thoughts or emotions. This is considered rigpa. It is so shockingly simple. This experience can occur quite easily, especially during sitting meditation, with the right instruction or guidance. At some point, when meditators become more familiar with the experience, then even formal sitting is not required. An individual can drop into this awareness anywhere, in any circumstances throughout the day.

The Flight of Garuda by Shabkar is a very popular Dzogchen text, loved for its profundity and clarity. He wrote the whole text in the form of songs. In one section, he describes the three kayas in the context of one's own awareness. He points out that the three kayas are just different states of our own awareness, or rigpa, and he demystifies rigpa. In Song 7, he says,

The three kayas (essence, nature, and compassion),
the five kayas, and the five primordial wisdoms,
if they are to be pointed out simultaneously,
directly by a finger,
then they are this present mind that is uncontrived,
not altered by conditions and not polluted by grasping,
clear and vivid awareness.

Here, he is basically saying rigpa, or awareness, is unbelievably simple. Whether or not you are sitting in the meditation posture, if you are ready, if you are not following your thoughts, if you just leave your mind alone, then what remains is the state of mind that is alert, spacious, clear, and aware. That is rigpa, that is awareness. In Dzogchen, the three kayas are just different states of that present awareness that can be realized in the context of one's own consciousness in the realm of here and now. In that sense, they are not abstract at all.

The very essence of that awareness—empty, no form, no color, no shape, no limitations—is the dharmakaya. Its nature is luminous; it is not blank nor dead; it is aware of itself, alert. That nature is the sambhogakaya. The dynamic energy from which thoughts, perceptions, and experiences arise is the nirmanakaya. The three kayas are described by the terms *essence*, *nature*, and *compassion*.

VERSE 2 - ESSENCE, NATURE, AND COMPASSION

Because the essence is empty, it is free from eternalism.
Its nature is luminous, therefore it is free from nihilism.
Its compassion is ceaseless, the ground of myriad emanations.
Even though it is divided into three, they are not separate
in actuality.
May I realize the true nature of the ground of Dzogchen.

This verse describes ground according to Dzogchen. In the commentary on the previous verse, we pointed out that there are wrong versions of ground called flawed zhi. This verse defines the true understanding of zhi, or ground, according to Dzogchen. One can safely say that Dzogchen has the most elaborate and refined explanation on zhi. It describes zhi in a way such that there won't be any kind of logical glitches or philosophical errors. Dzogchen masters tend to emphasize that zhi is ineffable and does not fall into eternalism or nihilism in any way. Not only that, Dzogchen sees that the ultimate truth in other systems is somehow tainted, either subtly or indirectly, by these two *isms*—eternalism and nihilism.

Here, this verse removes any possibility that ground could fall into the trap of eternalism or nihilism by using reasoning that can be called vajra-reasoning, or enlightened reasoning, because it is not like ordinary logic.

One of the reasons used here is that the three kayas are already present in ground. They explain this through pointing out that the very nature of what is called ground-rigpa, or *zhi rigpa* (W. *gzhi'i rig pa*), is the embodiment of the three kayas. Ground-rigpa itself is the nature of mind as well as primordial consciousness, the state of consciousness prior to anything else —prior to ego, prior to duality. Here the verse is saying that the very essence of ground-rigpa is empty; its nature is luminous; and its capacity is ceaseless. In the following paragraphs, we will explain those three principles as well as the Dzogchen version of the three kayas.

"Because the essence is empty, it is free from eternalism."

"The essence is empty" is pointing out that ground, or ground-rigpa, does not exist in a particular way. If something exists, we can point out what it is. But ground does not exist in any particular way that can be pointed to. It has no characteristics. Of course, it does not exist in matter, with shape, color, size, and so forth. It also does not exist as a mental reality that we construct with our concepts and ideas. It doesn't exist in the material or the mental world. It has no characteristics and cannot be defined by anything. The essence is considered the dharmakaya.

Negation

One of the few commentaries on this Dzogchen prayer is by Getse Pandita (Getse Gyurme Tsewang Chokdrub). He goes through the prayer line by line, using his ample academic knowledge to decipher the text and to quote from various

Tantric sutras and shastras. In his commentary, he described zhi as:

> ...no awareness, no unawareness, no Buddha, no sentient beings, no samsara, no nirvana, no light, no colors, no sacred forms, no wisdom, no ground, no path, no result, no delusion, no liberation, no imprisonment, no freedom, no karma, no klesha, no prana, no elements, no affirmation, no negation, nothing that ever existed, and nobody is there.

He is saying there is nothing to be referred to as existing. You cannot say zhi exists in this way or that way. There is no reference point, so you cannot find zhi existing in any forms, in any way.

Getse Pandita himself was a Longchen Nyingthig lineage holder and a close disciple of Dodrupchen Jigme Trinley Ozer, Jigme Lingpa's main disciple. The language he uses is not original. He is simply quoting the words and phrases from Dzogchen texts that cover this point about zhi. But it is very sharp and direct language that can help us "cut to the chase," because sometimes it can be hard for some people to relate to the traditional Dzogchen language.

It is very common to use language of negation to describe the highest truth in the Buddhist tradition. Here, "essence is empty" is negation. What is being negated? In this context, this aspect of zhi, the "essence is empty," is negating everything in existence, since zhi is the ground of all, not just ordinary things but even things that are held sacred, such as wisdom and sacred forms.

We see this type of negation in various sutras and tantras. Negation often helps us get rid of the idea of eternalism. Belief in eternalism has a logical consequence: the very thing that is eternal becomes part of the nature of reality. Then the nature of reality would be partial and finite, or even conditioned. It would definitely not be ineffable if its essence was eternal. If nirvana existed in the essence of zhi, then nobody would be deluded in the first place. There wouldn't be samsara or suffering, and there wouldn't be anyone who was lost or confused. Everyone would have been enlightened from the beginning. Similarly, if samsara existed as if it were part of the essence of the ground, then zhi would not be ineffable and delusion could never be transcended.

Try to imagine that zhi is a person, and your friend is going to introduce you to him or her. Imagine you never met with that person before. Somehow you have seen his or her picture and have all kinds of ideas about that person just based on seeing a picture. You have constructed notions about that person—their character, their habits, and so forth—yet none of them might be true. But just forming all these opinions becomes a hindrance to meeting the person. It could be so problematic that you might not allow yourself to really understand that person. If your friend who was introducing the two of you knew that your head was filled with all these opinions, your friend would help you empty your mind and drop any ideas about that person. Then there would be space in your mind. Through that empty space, there would be room for you to meet with that person and begin to learn who he or she is.

In some sense, this verse is like that. It is taking away every concept we have about zhi, especially any kind of reference point, to let us touch the aspect of zhi that is nonconceptual and ineffable. We are taking everything away, so we cannot think of zhi in any form, not samsara nor nirvana, not atoms nor molecules. There is nothing there.

The empty aspect of ground is not esoteric, not at all. Intuitively, such an insight can come spontaneously when we spend some time inquiring and working with questions like "Are things real or not?" Through that inquiry, we are automatically able to feel that our idea of reality is illusory. We feel there is not really a solid ground for anything. A suspicion grows in us that things don't exist as they appear. Naturally, through deep inquiry, we feel intuitively that there is something not completely correct about the way we see things. Usually we see everything as so real: there is me, there is the world out there, there is good, there is bad, this is my house, this is my body. It all seems so real. Yet this whole idea that things do not exist in the realm of the ineffable, zhi, makes sense to a lot of people when they deeply contemplate reality.

One time I was driving with a friend of mine from my home to Mendocino, a nearby town. We had a very intellectually stimulating conversation, so time flew by. We began to talk about what is real and what is not real. He was into computer programming, and he wondered if it was possible that there was some intelligent consciousness out there who created a virtual reality that we are part of. Of course, I didn't go along with that. But it dawned on me that people have an intuitive suspicion about reality and through either philosophy or scientific theories, they try to shatter the idea that their version of reality is real.

"Its nature is luminous, therefore it is free from nihilism."

But if one dwells on just this aspect of zhi—the essence is empty—one does not see the whole picture of zhi, since this could be misunderstood as nothingness, which is nihilism. So understanding the second aspect of zhi-rigpa, or ground-rigpa —its nature is luminous—ensures that we don't end up asserting that zhi-rigpa is nothingness. Even though ground-rigpa does not exist in any particular way and has no particular characteristics, it is not just purely nothingness. On the contrary, its nature is asserted as luminous.

This notion of luminosity, *osel* (W. *'od gsal*), is self-explanatory in that it automatically connotes that zhi is not nothingness. Imagine if you never studied about this notion in Buddhism. Hearing *luminous*, the last thing you would think would be nothingness. You might associate it with life, manifestation, beautiful images like rainbows or flowers, or divine presence. Luminosity, in Dzogchen, is a way of removing any possibility for our mind to interpret ground as nothingness. Beyond that, it is wise not to put too many concepts onto luminosity, not to get attached to a lot of preconceived notions about what it is, and not to reify it.

In Dzogchen, this luminosity is often described as sambhogakaya. As we said in the last chapter, Dzogchen describes the three kayas as aspects of the true nature of mind, so sambhogakaya fits as one of the three aspects. *Luminosity* means something is vivid and alive, not dead nor blank, and is also pure. Luminosity is more than a mind empty of limitations; it is an awareness that is alive and fully present. Sambhogakaya represents sacred life that is enriched with all the virtues and perfections. So sambhogakaya and the luminous aspect of awareness go together hand in hand.

"Its compassion is ceaseless, the ground of myriad emanations."

The third aspect, compassion, which once again describes another aspect of ground-rigpa, means ground has an extraordinary capacity from which the entire manifestation of ground can arise. This is what is meant by "compassion is ceaseless." We might wonder why they use the word *compassion.* The term is offering a sacred outlook on ground-rigpa. Otherwise, it would imply that everything arises from something trivial. Compassion has a sense of sacredness; it is almost a cosmic compassion. In this context, compassion is an honorific word for capacity. This is very positive. Compassion gives the sense that fundamentally ground, from which everything arises, has a flavor of goodness, since everything arises from that unceasing compassion. This compassion is often defined as the nirmanakaya in Dzogchen.

Together, all three kayas are complete, always present in ground-rigpa, which is one of the main premises of the Dzogchen Tantras. In many ways, Dzogchen's way of describing the three kayas is brilliant. Not only does it minimize any possibility of turning them into theistic deities, it is also more experiential and nondual. It is easier for us to relate to the three kayas since they are all about the true nature of our mind and consciousness. We can apply the Dzogchen model in our actual practice to better understand the nature of our mind. It is also less complicated. This is why Jigme Lingpa said in one of his writings that it is so liberating to talk about three kayas from the Dzogchen point of view, whereas he felt that the scholasticism of the Prajnaparamita system describing a complex model of three kayas and the path of the bhumis was exhausting.

Zhi Nang - Manifestation

**Now that zhi, or ground-rigpa, is described, we cannot just stop there, because zhi is related to the entire existence; it is how everything comes into being.

What comes after zhi is *zhi nang* (W. *gzhi snang*), manifestation of ground, or display of ground, which shows how the whole existence is manifested from that zhi. Even though the terms *zhi* and *zhi nang* sound very philosophical or abstract, they can be incorporated into our experience right now. The explanations of zhi and zhi nang will help us understand the nature of mind; why we experience the world of phenomena, thoughts, sensations, colors, and shapes; how we become deluded in the first place; and how we can be awakened, sometimes in a very spontaneous fashion. So we are not really talking about some impersonal, cosmic reality. Instead, these notions are a way of understanding who we are. Basically, zhi and zhi nang are a way to understand our consciousness and our own experience of reality. Let's look at two ways of explaining zhi nang.

Youthful Vase Body

When we describe how things manifest from ground, we have to use metaphorical language and images, or we can't imagine it. To explain how the whole existence manifests from zhi, Dzogchen writings use the metaphor of the *youthful vase body*, *zhön nu bum ku* (W. *gzhon nu bum sku*). This metaphor is one of the most often-used terms in Dzogchen writings. It has nothing to do with a divine physical body or the physical body of Buddha. Here, *body* refers to a formless dimension of ground-rigpa where it resides as *nang sel tra wé yéshé* (W. *nang gsal phra ba'i ye shes*), the inner luminosity-subtle primordial wisdom. This subtle wisdom is often described as dormant and not manifested outwardly.

Let's dissect the meaning of youthful vase body. *Youthful* means deathless, beyond all conditions. *Vase* here is metaphor for that which veils the luminosity.

Imagine there is a flame burning inside a clay vase. The flame is the inner luminosity, but no one can see its light shining out of the vase. Imagine suddenly the vase breaks. At that moment, the light shines.

In the metaphor, this inner luminosity is more than light —it is the very makeup of the existence that we perceive, which shines in that moment. It shines vividly in the form of five colored lights, which are the radiance of the inner luminosity-subtle primordial wisdom. These five colored lights emerge from the youthful vase body and become the entire manifestation. This is the emergence of zhi nang, or the display of ground, which shows how the whole existence that we perceive manifests from zhi.

This metaphor is much more profound than the phrase itself might sound. There is so much to explore and to be understood from this. Not only does it describe how all things arise in our perception in the first place, but everything that we are experiencing right now—sight, sound, form, world— are a display of our own mind. Ultimately, they are the manifestation of ground, so there is no duality between what we are experiencing as reality and our own mind. This is depicted in the metaphor, because the light that is shining from the vase is not coming from outside but is the radiance itself. The light of the flame within the vase before the vase breaks is the inner luminosity. And the light that shines out is what we experience. But they are not separate since they come from the same light. It is a beautiful metaphor to show that all our experiences are a display of our own mind or consciousness.

Eight Doorways

In the beginning, zhi nang appears from ground the way clouds suddenly appear from out of nowhere in a clear sky. The Dzogchen Tantras often talk about eight ways of spontaneously manifesting. They postulate that zhi nang appears through the eight gates, or eight doorways, of spontaneous presence, *lhün drup go gyé* (W. *lhun grub sgo brgyad*).

The first doorway is that zhi nang manifests as unobstructed compassion to all beings. The second doorway is the manifestation as lights. The third is manifesting as the kayas, and the fourth is manifesting as wisdom. The fifth is manifesting as nonduality, and the sixth is freedom from extremes. The seventh and eighth are the impure gate of samsara and the pure gate of wisdom. These eight doorways are quite precise but in order to understand the nuances, one might need further study of traditional Dzogchen texts. Even though each of the doorways is distinct, understanding the subtleties will help us understand the whole paradigm. On the other hand, as long as the essential meaning is understood, it's not necessary to try to figure out each gate or doorway. So here I will not offer a commentary on each one. Rather, the eight doorways convey the idea that even though primordial ground is singular, zhi nang can manifest in myriad displays, such as wisdom, kayas, realms of buddhas, suffering, happiness, and so forth.

So zhi nang is not singular but is as versatile as existence itself. *Eight doorways* means that zhi nang manifests in a versatile fashion with endless potentiality. They are called doorways because if you realize zhi nang is purely the display of awareness itself, then zhi nang becomes a doorway to enlightenment. But if you haven't realized this and project the display outside of yourself, then zhi nang becomes a doorway to delusion or samsara.

Zhi nang has never been separate from zhi, ground. But there is also a natural dissolution state where all the zhi nang dissolve back into primordial ground. Everything we perceive as the phenomenal world is just the pure display of awareness, which dissolves back into itself. The insight or wisdom that recognizes this becomes the highest fruition, or enlightenment.

Another Explanation of Zhi Nang

Another way of explaining zhi nang is like this: In that primordial ground, our pure awareness, or our original consciousness, is awakened by what is called the life force, *so lung* (W. *srog rlung*). Then the moment it wakes up, it wakes up as this extraordinary phenomenon...that's all we can say. Phenomenon is a very safe word to use, because it doesn't have any connotation of being good or bad, holy or ordinary. Original consciousness wakes up, and then it begins to experience its own display, which is sometimes called the display of primordial ground, or zhi nang. Consciousness doesn't stay in a flat state of just being aware of something, but instead, it has an extraordinary, dynamic potential from which its own display comes into being: thought, colors, shapes, and so forth. As we said in the previous explanation, they often say five colors emerge, and then the whole world of phenomena—this unbelievable, immeasurable, myriad display of primordial ground—comes into our experience. And yet the entire existence remains none other than the display of ground itself. They are not separate from each other.

The arising of zhi nang is a very critical moment. If the whole existence arises as a display of ground itself, it would be fine, but it is the moment when awareness and unawareness take place. This is also the moment where nirvana and samsara come into being in our consciousness. It is a very crucial moment. At this moment, consciousness has two potentials. It has the potential to be enlightened but also has the potential to be deluded. It can go either way. Sometimes it goes to freedom, and sometimes it goes to imprisonment. This is something we can see happening in everyday life.

When consciousness makes the choice to use its potential for freedom, then consciousness realizes that this whole thing is its own self-display, *rang nang (W. rang snang)*. Consciousness realizes that everything it is witnessing is not some kind of intrinsically existent, objective reality but its own experience. And that awakening is sometimes called Buddha Samantabhadra in the Dzogchen Tantras or Samantabhadri, whatever gender you would like to use, although they have nothing to do with gender. Buddha Samantabhadra and Samantabhadri are not some kind of historical figures, as we have already said. They are just different expressions of that radical, immediate awakening.

So this is also a moment when the primordial Buddha Samantabhadra becomes enlightened. In the moment that zhi nang emerges from zhi, Samantabhadra, without going through any process of purification or performing good deeds, realizes that the whole manifestation is none other than the display of its own awareness. With that recognition, according to Dzogchen, Buddha Samantabhadra becomes enlightened.

Once again, it is important not to regard Samantabhadra as some lucky person who won the lottery. Samantabhadra here is an impersonal awakening or awareness. The whole thing is a representation of enlightenment or awareness itself, which does not belong to one person. Obviously, there is awakening in the universe. Manifestation and enlightenment happen simultaneously. There is no manifestation without enlightenment.

Most importantly, we can remember that our consciousness always has full potential, and we have a choice in each and every moment not to descend but to ascend, not to go down but to go high. The choice is always there.

Here, some readers may wonder if this is like a history of the universe, or if we are talking about how the nature of consciousness becomes awakened or deluded. The answer is that this is not a history of the universe. The reason I am making such a statement is because in the modern world when someone comes across these Dzogchen ideas, they may sound like a description of how the whole universe comes into being. But this is not like the *Old Testament* of Dzogchen. This is about how one's own, or anyone's, reality comes into being.

When I say "one's own reality," I am talking about the life or reality that we experience individually. When we lie down on the ground at night and look at the Milky Way, we can feel that we are seeing the universe. Unless you are an astronaut, this is one of the easiest ways to expand and not be lost in the nitty-gritty of daily life. We all have earthly, mundane duties and problems centered around our individual life. In a moment of looking at the stars, we glimpse something bigger than our own individual reality.

But even then, you are experiencing your own reality, because you are the one who is witnessing it. When you feel you are stuck in the kitchen washing dishes, that is like a small version of your own reality, and you are the one who is experiencing that. When you look up to the sky and feel something vast, your mind may think it is the cosmos or universe. But still, you are the one who is experiencing it. So it is just a bigger version of your own reality. When you don't look up at night—perhaps you are busy watching TV at home, or munching on something—the Milky Way might be there, but in your mind, the Milky Way doesn't exist at that moment. So everything is all your own reality—beauty, ugliness, holy, profane, infinite, finite. Everything you experience is your own reality. In that sense, the zhi nang that you are witnessing is your own reality.

Therefore, some Dzogchen masters make a subtle distinction between *rang nang*, one's own reality, versus the collective reality. In a moment of dissolution of zhi nang that happens during a powerful spiritual awakening, or even naturally during an extraordinary occasion, during meditation, or the bardo, the zhi nang that dissolves in that moment is one's own reality, rang nang. That does not mean the collective reality dissolves in that moment. While you are experiencing dissolution, perhaps everyone else is either enjoying zhi nang or getting bogged down in it.

Zhi and zhi nang are neither personal nor impersonal. This is a truly important point to bear in mind. The moment we somehow interpret them either way, we are losing our grip on this big view of Dzogchen. Our mind has a tendency to make these things personal or impersonal, since this is what we have been doing all along. This is a very old tendency.

Unawareness Arises

Once zhi nang, the display of ground, arises, then there are two possibilities. One is the insight that recognizes zhi nang as none other than the display of one's own awareness. The other possibility is the opposite of that, which is not being able to recognize it. That state of nonrecognition is known as *avidya* in Sanskrit, which is often described as the genesis of samsara. The interpretation of avidya in various tenets or doctrines is not always singular or universal. Sometimes definitions of avidya are slightly different from each other and may have different nuances. In Dzogchen, there are three kinds of unawareness, which we will describe later.

It would be nice if unawareness didn't happen at the moment zhi nang arises. That may be something we wish for now and then. But unawareness happens as part of the whole grand picture. Without it, there would not be samsara, there would not be unenlightened beings, and there would not even be a path. How could there be a path if there was no suffering to transcend? There wouldn't be sentient beings who are deluded.

If there was no delusion in the first place, you wouldn't even be here today reading this book, trying to understand the path of Dzogchen. Instead, you might be living in a perfect utopian world, enjoying good food, running on the beach, and always being ecstatic. The reason we are interested in the path is that there is a desire in each of us to be awakened. To be awakened means not to be deluded. Hopefully, we can open our hearts and recognize our delusion without feeling bad. Delusion basically means being lost in our mind, in our emotions, our feelings, our thoughts. The path is about sentient beings who are deluded and are trying to be liberated.

If unawareness never happened, everyone would be enlightened from the beginning. That may sound like a tempting hypothesis, but it has a lot of logical holes. One of my friends said that suffering is a rich ingredient of life, because it makes us more human and compassionate, more ripened and baked, otherwise we would be happy vegetables. I would add that if everyone was enlightened from the beginning, the whole universe would be like a heaven of happy vegetables. It may not be very interesting in the long run.

In short, unawareness in this context is not being able to recognize that zhi nang is the display of one's own awareness. Therefore, in Dzogchen, people often quote this line from the *Prayer of Buddha Samantabhadra*, which is excerpted from the *Tantra of the Great Perfection that Reveals the All-Penetrating Wisdom Mind of Samantabhadra,* revealed by the great Dzogchen master Rigdzin Godem:

> *One ground, two paths, two fruitions.*

This turns out to be a very condensed and profound verse, which encapsulates the entirety of the Tantrayana and Dzogchen teachings.

It is the "one ground" because it is not divided; it is neither good nor bad. You cannot say this ground is enlightened or unenlightened, wholesome or unwholesome, blissful or painful. At the same time, almost all your experiences—happiness, sorrow, liberation, delusion—all arise from this very ground.

"Two paths" refers to awareness and unawareness. Rigdzin Godem is saying that in the end, there are only two states of your consciousness, which simplifies everything. He said if we look into our own mind, we will see only two mental states. Everything else is just an expression of these two mental states, which turn out to be awareness and unawareness.

"Two fruitions" are samsara and nirvana, imprisonment and liberation. This is a general description of how in the beginning, awareness and unawareness emerge in conjunction with each other from zhi, or ground.

Unawareness is the very foundation of all our pain and misery. As long as unawareness continues, our suffering and misery will continue. Not only that, we will continue to create pain for ourselves and for the world, too, without even recognizing what we are doing. In general, unawareness is described as the genesis of samsara, delusion, and suffering. This theory is shared among all the schools of thought, such as the Sutrayana and Tantrayana. Although the schools of thought describe unawareness using different definitions and various categories, one common way to describe how samsara comes into being is through the twelve links of interdependent origination, the first of which is unawareness, or avidya.

Avidya is a useful concept that doesn't have a heavy-handed doctrine associated with it. In the Western tradition, the idea of original sin can be a very heavy concept if it is misunderstood. But in Eastern spirituality, the concept of original sin does not exist. There is only original unawareness, avidya. Original unawareness is not a sin; it is purely innocent. It is just not awakened. That's it. There's nothing impure or bad about original unawareness. It's just like sleeping. When you fall asleep, would you say sleep is sinful or impure? We would not usually say sleep is sinful, impure, or bad. No scripture or any kind of logic proves that sleep is a sin. Not at all. It is innocent. So even original unawareness is not intrinsically a vice. It is an innocent forgetfulness of who we are in our true nature. That's avidya, or *tok mé ma rigpa* (W. *thog ma'i ma rig pa*), original unawareness.

Three Kinds of Unawareness

Dzogchen texts often go further to give a more subtle understanding of unawareness, and in doing so, three kinds of unawareness or *ma rigpa sum* (W. *ma rig pa gsum*) are defined. The three kinds of unawareness become the catalyst that gives rise to samsara, to the world of internal delusion and suffering. They are not just abstract concepts, old philosophy, or mental constructs. They can be understood in relationship to our own mind. These categories are very understandable. We can use them to see our own unawareness, to see how our own consciousness gets deluded; how our own mind gets immersed in delusion, ideas, and concepts; and ultimately, how we suffer.

First Unawareness

The first unawareness is known as "causal unawareness of single identity," *gyu dak nyi chik pé ma rigpa* (W. *rgyu bdag nyid gcig pa'i ma rig pa*). People use different terms to translate this into English. The first unawareness serves as the basis of the two other kinds of unawareness. In some sense, it could be regarded as the genesis of all unawareness, and that is why it is called "causal" unawareness.

At the moment when zhi nang arises from zhi, consciousness arises with the ability to be aware and to recognize. Consciousness could go in any direction with that ability. It could be awakened at that moment, knowing that whatever it experiences is not coming from outside and is just a display of itself. Or consciousness could get trapped by reifying its own experience of reality. There is always the potential for consciousness to become ignorant and deluded, regardless of whether consciousness is experiencing anything or not. That potential is called unawareness, but it is not literally unawareness in the way we understand the word *unawareness*; it is the potential.

One's whole experience of reality can be regarded as a grand show that is happening in the realm of awareness itself. This means rigpa has the potential or energy from which the whole phenomenal reality can emerge—samsara, nirvana, sorrow, joy, good, bad, past, future—while it is all really none other than the display of awareness itself. So one could say that the first unawareness is present all along. It is not a separate entity from ground and does not have a separate identity from ground. Therefore, it is called "single identity."

As an analogy, there is a light in front of where I am sitting right now. Behind this light is a switch that I can turn left or right. If I turn it to one side, the light becomes dim. But if I turn the switch in the other direction, then the light becomes brighter and brighter. So in some sense, you could say that this lamp in front of me has the potential to become illuminated, which allows me to read books with it, find things, and so forth. It can also become completely dark. I can turn it off. It has all this potential. And the switch comes with the lamp itself; it is not a separate thing that you buy.

The first unawareness of single identity is like the potential to turn off the light; in other words, the first unawareness of single identity is the potential to be deluded. The aspect of our mind that is lacking in wisdom is the unawareness of single identity. The first unawareness is the idea that unless our mind is fully awakened, fully imbued with wisdom and insight, it has all the potential to descend and be lost in its own traps, concepts, ideas, and illusions.

Second Unawareness

When consciousness emerged from zhi, it didn't recognize itself. The moment it emerged, simultaneously it didn't recognize itself. Then according to Dzogchen, with that state of non-recognition, consciousness becomes aware of whatever is unfolding in its own field, the whole world of phenomena, thoughts, experiences, emotions, colors, shapes, patterns, and movement. But then consciousness does not recognize that this whole experience, the world of phenomena, is its own display. That lack of recognition is the second unawareness, labeled as inborn unawareness, or co-emergent unawareness, *lhen chik kyé pé ma rigpa* (W. *lhan cig skyes pa'i ma rig pa*). It is co-emergent because it happens right there when consciousness emerges.

Often they describe that inborn unawareness is a state that has no remembrance or insight. For example, the extraordinary Dzogchen liturgy, *The Prayer of Buddha Samantabhadra,* which we quoted earlier, says co-emergent unawareness is that state in which consciousness is lacking in mindfulness, or remembrance, and is distracted. How simple this definition is. There is consciousness, which is kind of aware of what is happening, but it has no mindfulness and doesn't really know what is happening. It doesn't know that the whole experience is just its own display.

Even though the three kinds of unawareness formulate how the world of duality, or samsara, comes into being from pure ground, they are also very applicable in everyday life and describe how we can get deluded.

For example, in everyday life, there is a state of consciousness in us that is similar to the second unawareness, where remembrance or mindfulness is lacking. As a result, we are often lost in our experiences. This unawareness is hard to recognize, because there is no specific thought, emotion, or delusion present. It often operates as a sneaky unawareness underneath our daily consciousness. If it were not there, we would not get lost in our experience in the first place. If there was anger, that would be obvious. You can feel that your being is contracted, and if the anger is strong, your heart rate goes up, your blood circulates faster, and people around you even recognize it. Often it doesn't feel good. Whereas the second unawareness is not like that. It is totally subtle, but it operates constantly and is a very powerful force that can drive your consciousness down. When we practice awareness or mindfulness, such unawareness is dissolved, or at least it is on our radar. That's why it is important to practice awareness or mindfulness even when you are not having any kind of troubled thoughts or emotions. In those states, you might tell yourself, "Now I am feeling pretty good, so I don't have to be in awareness." While that sounds logical, the subtle unawareness will sooner or later become fertile ground for delusion.

Third Unawareness

The third unawareness is unawareness of labeling. When zhi nang arises, consciousness, because it didn't recognize everything was its own display, separated itself. Now it begins labeling and perceiving through the lens of duality—self, other, here, there, good, bad. From that, all the rest develops: ego; the kleshas, or inner poisons; and all of samsara, the world of suffering.

So the third unawareness is called *kün tak kyi ma rigpa* (W. *kun brtags kyi ma rig pa*), or unawareness of mental designation. Not only does consciousness not recognize this whole experience of reality as its own display, but consciousness begins to label everything and misperceive that everything is outside itself. Consciousness begins to create the duality between oneself and one's own display as a reality out there, the outside world. Then consciousness designates itself as "me" or the observer, the experiencer, or the self, and the entire world of duality comes into being. This is how ego comes into being, even though the whole thing is just a display of consciousness itself.

Consciousness becomes very attached to this whole mistaken perception, starts reifying everything, and eventually falls into the trap of hope and fear, aversion and attraction. Consciousness experiences aversion towards one thing by misperceiving that object as out there and real, and it starts hating that object, even though the object is merely its own projection. Then consciousness becomes very attached to another phenomenon even though that phenomenon is also its own display.

This is called unawareness of mental designation, a state of mind where you are totally lost in your thoughts, and you believe the thoughts and stories in your mind.

Some scholars describe the three kinds of unawareness this way: If you are in deep sleep, and you are not aware of anything, that is like the first unawareness, ignorance of same identity. Then you wake up suddenly, maybe rubbing your eyes. You don't see clearly. Some movement is happening, but you can't really recognize things. That is like the co-emergent unawareness. And then you wake up more fully, and you start labeling everything in your bedroom—that's my bookshelf, that's my smartphone, and that's my jacket. This is how the unawareness of mental designation works.

These three kinds of unawareness are regarded as the root of samsara. We can use the categories to recognize the unawareness in our own consciousness. For example, you may be sitting in your living room, everything is okay, the temperature is perfect; you are drinking delicious tea and listening to lovely music. Not so much is going on in your mind. But you can still be controlled by inborn unawareness. A thought arises. It could be anything. "My life is not working," which is a totally wild story that has no truth. Unless we are in awareness, our tendency is to immediately believe that thought and turn that thought into reality, when it is simply mind's game. This happens all the time. Everyone is always believing their thoughts unless they are meditating. It is so painful to believe our mind, even for a few moments. Sometimes I wonder how people can live in this world every day while they are believing their mind constantly from the moment they wake up until they fall asleep. It is amazing that people are able to live with relative peace and not go crazy. These days, we may be witnessing that people are lost in their minds perhaps more than ever. Sometimes we can easily see how much we humans are lost in our belief systems and ideas, which cause so much suffering.

There is logic in Buddhism that says unless you understand delusion, you will not understand wisdom. Unless you understand unawareness, you will not understand awareness. This is inconvenient logic for the spiritual ego, which would like to go directly to awareness and not talk about unawareness. It's like thinking, "I want to realize nonduality and I don't want to know anything about duality." But Buddhist logic says unless we know what unawareness is, we will not easily know awareness. So it is helpful to talk about these three forms of unawareness as well as the kleshas in general. This is also why there is so much explanation about the kleshas in almost every Buddhist system, such as Abhidharma.

In some sense, the distinction between the three kinds of unawareness may sound subtle or abstract. But the point is that unawareness is in each of us until our mind is completely awakened or insightful. Sometimes these three kinds of unawareness can be identified empirically. Their individual characteristics are described in the Dzogchen writings, but the language is very subtle. It needs a lot of reflection to understand.

On the other hand, we don't want to be too hooked into the Dzogchen philosophy, which could become a hindrance to the actual experience. It's possible one could have authentic awakening through practicing Dzogchen without knowing all these subtle theoretical points. Therefore, it is important not to get hung up on remembering the definitions of these three kinds of unawareness.

Experiential, not Philosophical

Again, one thing to keep in mind is that unawareness is not considered bad, negative, or unwholesome. It is not some kind of original sin. It simply has the starring role in the development of the world of samsara.

This whole description of unawareness is really quite psychological. The three kinds of unawareness are not just abstract, philosophical notions but are experiential. You can use the Dzogchen system in your everyday life to see how your own consciousness becomes deluded through the development of the three kinds of unawareness. The more we become aware of the ways or process of falling into the trap of unawareness, the more we are able to carry awareness and insight in everyday life.

Unawareness is actually very simple to recognize. It comes from not looking into our own mind. When we don't turn our mind towards itself, then there is unawareness. This is why the Dzogchen masters always say, look at your own mind. This is a phrase they use again and again. "Look at your own mind." Sometimes they say this is the highest teaching they can give. This is ultimately the most profound practice. It's the secret of enlightenment. The Dzogchen masters always say, in the end, the Dharma, the spiritual teaching, is unbelievably simple. The idea of looking at your own mind is unbelievably simple. There's no doctrine, there's no concept, there's no philosophy, there's no *ism* in it. How simple it is. Sometimes it sounds so simple that it doesn't entice us. There are other spiritual things that entice us more than this idea of looking at our own mind. But the moment we look at our own mind, there is already awareness. Awareness is the lamp or the light of consciousness that illuminates everything.

Both awareness and unawareness are neither intrinsically real nor are they diametrically opposite. Consciousness sometimes goes to sleep, which is unawareness, and consciousness wakes up, which is awareness, but they are both the display of the same consciousness. It's like me—if I am asleep or awake, I am the same person. It's not like there are two different individuals. No doubt the experience is very different being asleep or being awake. I might be very unconscious or have dreams, hopefully nice ones, but then when I am awake, the whole experience changes. I have a very strong experience of the senses; I can act, move, speak, and interact with the physical world. But I am the same person—there are not two different people. In the same way, consciousness is sometimes waking up to reality and sometimes falling asleep in the bed of unawareness. We call them awareness and unawareness but it is just consciousness going through its own states.

VERSE 3 - INCONCEIVABLE GROUND

Inconceivable and free from all conceptual exaggerations,
The reference point to existent or nonexistent collapses.
Even Buddha's tongue struggles to describe this truth.
It has no beginning, no end, and no middle. It is a space
of deep, profound clarity.
May I realize the true nature of the ground of Dzogchen.

"Inconceivable" is an expression that is used in Tantric Buddhism, especially in relationship to the ultimate truth. The idea of inconceivable is that ultimate truth is all-pervasive and is the nature of all things. Inconceivable has the connotation of going beyond words and concepts. More than that, it refers to something that it is utterly profound and vast, way bigger than the scope of our thinking mind.

Here, it would be useful to talk about the idea of the two truths: the relative truth and the ultimate truth. Even though some readers already know this, it is important to restate that the two truths have nothing to do with a duality between sublime versus ordinary, good versus bad.

Two Truths

The notions of relative truth and ultimate truth are a brilliant way of solving a philosophical dilemma: if there were only ultimate truth, everything else—all the earthly reality—would have to be denied, which not only sounds nihilistic but also doesn't make sense. Everything that we are experiencing is real to a certain extent. Obviously, there is a physical reality. For example, the house where we live and the physical body that we can feel are not just mental constructs. Look around at your table, your carpet, your dining room, your family members, and so forth. They are real in many ways, and we need these mental constructs to relate to things. We need ideas like "this is my house, this is my neighbor's house," for example. Life would be quite chaotic without these mental constructs. If we didn't have mental constructs, the whole world would descend into some kind of nebulous chaos. Lots of people in the past misunderstood the meaning of ultimate truth. Yes, ultimate truth transcends earthly reality, but some people took it too far and thought that you cannot have ultimate truth unless the relative truth was totally rejected.

There are wild stories about this. Once a lama was expounding on the ultimate truth to his students, saying, "There's nothing here—no you, no me, it's all illusion." One student thought he understood it, and he went back home. The student was a yogi, and usually yogis have a vow of *ahimsa*, nonviolence, and don't take the lives of any beings. Although the main food in the old days was dairy and meat, many yogis were vegetarian and didn't take the life of animals. But this yogi picked up a knife and began slaughtering a sheep. People were shocked. But he said, "Well, there is no sheep, there is no "I" to slaughter it." The yogi didn't understand the absolute truth and totally rejected the relative truth. He turned the absolute truth into a "thing," a pseudo-transcendence.

So the two truths have to be brought into the teaching context so we can have an authentic understanding of the ultimate truth. Without the relative truth, the ultimate truth can be a dangerous concept, leading to nihilism and outright rejection of the obvious reality.

So what is the difference between the relative truth and the ultimate truth? The difference is that relative truth is a version of reality that is agreed upon by everyone. It is the version of reality that allows us to have a sense of right, wrong, good, bad, as well as practical matters. That's why Buddha himself said he did not deny anything. There was perhaps doubt among people when Buddha started teaching emptiness. When he said things are empty of true identity, some people might have thought he was rejecting earthly reality. But Buddha made this famous statement: "I don't debate with the world; the world debates with me." He is saying that as far as relative truth is concerned, he would not reject anything. He would agree with the conceptual system of reality that is held by the world. Buddha does not reject anything. But when it comes to the ultimate truth, Buddha uses negation. He negated almost everything in the sutras.

So we need the relative truth as well as the ultimate truth. Imagine that you are somewhere in a town near New York City. A tourist is lost and asks you how to get to New York City. If you answer that question from ultimate truth because you were reading all the texts on nonduality, and you say, "There's no New York City… it's an illusion," that would not be the right answer.

It is true that in deep inquiry, New York City is just a concept, because it didn't exist at some point in history. Then the settlers arrived, laid out the borders, started developing it, and eventually it was called New York City, becoming "the" city. There is no inherent demarcation for New York City from the point of view of the ultimate truth. But in the relative truth, there is a place called New York City.

In Dzogchen, the ultimate truth even transcends the law of karma. So relative truth is needed, especially to bring in the law of karma, cause and effect, even if it is transcended in the ultimate truth. The law of karma has to be there. It doesn't fit in the framework of ultimate truth but it naturally fits in the framework of relative truth.

Ultimate Truth

But the problem is that the world in general is not awakened to the ultimate truth. When the Buddha said, "The world debates with me," he was referring to the general population that is caught up only in the relative truth. They don't think it is relative truth; they think it is the only truth. If they could say "relative truth," they would have a sense of comparison to the ultimate, but their view of reality is the only reality for them. So "the world debates with me" refers to the fact that the majority of people are not in touch with the ultimate truth.

Therefore, spiritual awakening describes those who have the direct experience of the ultimate truth. They are called exalted ones, *arya*, because they are unique and rare. If everyone was awakened, they wouldn't be considered exalted. They are rare because it is challenging to have the courage to question the reality that is held by everyone else. Even if someone has an intellectual understanding of the big truth that goes beyond the consensus reality, it is extremely difficult to truly live that unless someone becomes an *arya*. There could be an intellectual understanding of the ultimate truth in the back of our minds but we would still easily fall into the version of reality constructed by the masses in some cases. This situation is depicted in the famous tale about a king.

Once there was a king who often consulted with astrologers on the affairs of the kingdom. One day the astrologer predicted that on the seventh day there would be rain, and whoever drank water from then on would become crazy. The king didn't want to become crazy so he covered his well so that the rain would not go inside. Nobody else knew about this prediction. The rain came down, and as the astrologer predicted, when everyone drank the water, they all became crazy except for the king. But as time went by, the way the king acted and what he said was very different from everyone else. People in the kingdom started calling the king "the crazy one." It seemed they might eventually plan to topple the king, and perhaps he was attached to his power. Out of such desperation to remain king, he drank the regular water, and he too became crazy, which was normal in the eyes of everyone else.

This tale is chilling because not only does it point out that collectively, the human world is run by delusion, totally oblivious to the ultimate truth, but it also points out that it is not easy to wake up. The force of the world holding us back to delusion is somehow stronger than the force to wake up. We need to bear that in mind.

Even before one has direct experience, if one starts to question and doubt whether the conventional reality is all there is, the seeds of awakening are planted in one's consciousness. The great second-century Indian master Aryadeva said even those who have doubt are already tearing down samsaric existence. It means when you think, "Is the whole thing really true?" you are already on the right path. Many people whom we regard as great thinkers and adepts are those who had this kind of doubt, who were able to question conventional reality, the reality believed by the consensus of people.

Without the wisdom of the ultimate truth, everything is so real, concrete, and heavy. Everything seems reified. That's why there is so much suffering in the world. There is heaviness in general, even energetically, just being incarnate, being human. Everything is compartmentalized between right and wrong, this and that. It seems heavy. The story behind all of our suffering seems to be an infallible truth. There's no crack in the story. There's a rigidity in our life. If there's someone who doesn't change their mind, we call them rigid. As a species, we human beings can sometimes be quite rigid.

Yet the truth is that life doesn't have to be so heavy. This whole life could be very light and celebratory. As human beings, there is always a choice to be free from the sense of heaviness, sometimes immediately, and feel *guyang lobde* (W. *gu yangs blo bde*). *Guyang* means spacious or carefree. *Lobde* means happy. It has the connotation of being happy unconditionally.

Guyang lobde is a Tibetan phrase that is often found in the teachings of nonconceptual Dharma such as Dzogchen. It can have different levels of understanding in an ordinary sense as well as in the context of the higher nondual teachings. This is also a way to describe the enlightened state of mind, even though the phrase sounds very simple. Buddhism has a very rich language to describe the enlightened state as well as the path to such an awakened state of consciousness. The sutra teachings often describe enlightenment with terms and concepts that are more philosophical, whereas Dzogchen often describes it with more nonconceptual language, the language of a *kusali,* someone who is truly free inside.

In a casual way, *guyang lobde* means being carefree, happy-go-lucky, relaxed without internal worry or conflict. But in the context of Dzogchen, it is the experience of being awakened. That amazing feeling of guyang lobde comes from having some direct awakening, an experiential understanding of the ultimate truth where all our concepts are no longer functioning. Our concepts, our story lines of who we are, are transcended. There is no more heaviness in our heart. Of course, this is true when you have the direct experience of that enlightened state. But even having just the theory of the ultimate truth will definitely bring one so much freedom. So it is most worthwhile to be invested in the ultimate truth.

"Inconceivable and free from all conceptual exaggerations,"

In this verse, zhi is described as "inconceivable," which is a word used again and again in Tantric Buddhism to describe the ultimate truth. "Inconceivable" does not mean that it is some kind of philosophically profound notion that only some great scholars or brilliant minds can understand. "Inconceivable" means that in general, it lies beyond the horizon of our intellectual mind, and that no perfect word can describe ground in this context.

One of the tantras says:

The inconceivable nature of reality—
The insightful one who has its meaning,
The siddhi is close to her.
Or the fool who has steadfast devotion,
The siddhi of union is close to her.
The intellectual one who analyzes and investigates,
The siddhi of accomplishment is far away from her.

The tantra is saying that the ultimate truth is so inconceivable that it is not something we can be smart about. Obviously we cannot outsmart it by being intelligent, analytical, or calculating. It is true that we can use our analytical intelligence to figure out a lot of things in the world. It is true that in all our human affairs, we can use our intelligence. But that is not true for the ultimate truth.

In some sense, the notion that the ultimate truth is inconceivable is standard in the Mahayana tradition. For example, Nagarjuna made the famous statement, "I have no assertions, therefore I am flawless." Nagarjuna thought that all the schools in Buddhism and beyond have some kind of ideology that they are very attached to. Their ideological assertion may have elements of eternalism or nihilism, but everyone is attached to some kind of doctrine. Nagarjuna saw all doctrines as some kind of mental elaboration, *trö pa* (W: *spros pa*), in that they do not hold truth in the realm of the nature of reality. In the end, he transcended all assertions. For him, that seems to be the highest point beyond which you cannot go, as far as ultimate truth is considered.

"The reference point to existent or nonexistent collapses."

Since ground is inexpressible, in the realm of the ultimate truth, ground is also neither existent nor nonexistent. If you assert that ground is existent, then ground is no longer ineffable, and that very assertion is a form of eternalism. On the other hand, if you assert ground as nonexistent, that statement is nihilistic. The nature of ground is the ultimate truth and transcends any kind of philosophical assertions. This aspiration prayer points out directly that any assertions are limiting. If ground is interpreted as existent, then ground is limited to being finite. If ground is described as nonexistent, then it is a rejection of the relative truth.

There is no reference point, no mental description of the ultimate truth. That's why you could say the ultimate truth is ineffable. At the same time, while Dzogchen points out that the ultimate truth is inconceivable or ineffable, it is also establishing itself as a system that does not fall into the two extremes of eternalism and nihilism. It's obvious that this aspiration prayer is emphatic about ensuring that we know that the nature of ground is nonconceptual and cannot be captured as finite or conceived of as a "thing."

There is no doubt that Dzogchen has a unique way of describing the ultimate truth as ineffable. But it is not only Dzogchen that describes the ultimate truth as ineffable. Other systems, such as Madhyamaka, do this as well. It seems that the idea that the ultimate truth is ineffable was commonly held in the Tibetan Buddhist tradition in regard to the Mahayana and Vajrayana doctrine until the popularity of Lama Tsongkhapa's writings, after which this idea was no longer widely held. This is why some scholars postulate two schools of thought: the Early Tibetan school and the Late Tibetan school (meaning thinkers before and after Lama Tsongkhapa's influence). Those in the Late Tibetan school do not subscribe to the idea that the ultimate truth is ineffable. The Nyingma, Kagyu, and Sakya traditions are considered part of the Early Tibetan School and do hold that the ultimate truth is ineffable. The terms *Early* and *Late* Tibetan schools are used in writings, for example, of Gendun Choepel, who wrote critically about those who could not accept the idea of the ineffable.

"Even Buddha's tongue struggles to describe this truth."

Yet there are no assertions that truly capture the ineffability of the ultimate truth. It is impossible to find the perfect word or concept that can describe zhi. The only way we can be awakened to zhi is by leaving the thinking mind—the intellect—behind and using a nonconceptual state of consciousness. Here, this verse says even Buddha's tongue has a hard time expressing it. This is a kind of humorous but shocking statement. Often in the minds of Buddhists, buddhas are awakened, have extraordinary wisdom, and are able to express the ultimate truth. They are like divine experts on the ultimate truth. It would be like saying Einstein has trouble describing the theory of relativity. However, the ultimate truth is beyond words, such that even Buddha cannot express it.

There are many stories about how great masters point out that the ineffable is beyond words. One vivid story describes a time when Buddha was ready to give a sermon, and most probably, people were waiting for this great sage to say something very profound. But he didn't utter one word. Then

Buddha held up a flower, and Mahakashyapa and Buddha exchanged smiles. They understood each other with perfect silent communication. Through this exchange, Buddha demonstrates that the ultimate truth is beyond words.

But the question is, if the truth is ineffable, can it be realized by us? Of course, the answer is absolutely yes. But the way of gaining insight into it may not be through the usual modus operandi of the intellectual mind. For example, something that is neither existent nor nonexistent is outside of the radar of the intellectual mind, which has a hard time figuring it out. This is why Dzogchen often says that the profound wisdom of Buddha cannot be realized through words, concepts, or texts but by relying on the pith instructions of a skilled master. Because it is so nonconceptual, sometimes symbols or gestures might be the last resort to enable someone to glimpse the ultimate truth.

This is depicted in the life of Mahamudra master Saraha, a great scholar who was also a monk for a long time. He became dissatisfied with his monastic training and scholasticism and wound up becoming a wandering yogi. He attributed his awakening to a woman who later became his consort. Once when he was traveling, he ran into the woman at a market. She was holding an arrow, sitting in a perfect posture without looking around. She closed one eye and pulled the arrow back as if she were ready to let it go to hit a target. They began a conversation, and the woman said, "The wisdom of Buddha can be understood through symbols and skillful means but not through words and letters." Saraha understood immediately the significance of this. It was about shooting the arrow of nonduality into the target of duality. In that moment, he had a profound awakening. His writing is deeply influenced by this awakening, and he often puts down the ability of the intellect and words when it comes to the ineffable. This anecdote vividly shows, as many of the nondual traditions often teach, that words and concepts will fail to bring us the taste, the real flavor, of the ultimate truth.

"It has no beginning, no end, and no middle. It is a space of deep, profound clarity."

In general, everything that exists physically and in our mental world can fall under the category of either conditioned or unconditioned. Almost every reality we live out is part of the conditioned. If you look around, everything you see or believe is conditioned. *Conditioned* means that things come into being through causes and conditions, and they have characteristics, limitations, and a history. When you look around, everything has a beginning, end, and middle, because everything exists in the context of time and the law of cause and effect. Yet the idea that something has a beginning and an end is just something that our mind designated. Whereas the ultimate is unconditioned, which means it transcends all these—characteristics, history, and time. There is no beginning, no end, and no in-between. But this does not mean it is eternal.

This verse transcends every possibility that ground could somehow be conditioned. The moment it has a beginning, end, or middle, then it has some kind of limitation. When we say "no beginning, no end," it's easy for the mind to think that ground is some supreme or eternal thing, because often the term *ground* or *ultimate truth* creates an image in our mind of something transcendental, heavenly, or divine. Dzogchen masters know this misunderstanding happens quite often, so they always make sure that people do not misconstrue the notion of zhi.

I heard a story about a lama who was teaching Dzogchen in the West. One time, the lama gave a teaching and then sent the students away with an assignment, asking everyone to meditate, to inquire into the nature of mind, to look for the nature of mind. When everyone came back, the lama was curious to know what they found. So he asked a few people, and they all found "something"—a blue-colored Buddha, or a beautiful vision with lights, or a double vajra. He was kind of shocked, since traditionally the answer is, "I haven't found anything." So he brought the sharing to a close, because he saw that people had misunderstood the teaching.

One reason people automatically turn the expressions *ground*, *nature of mind*, or *Buddha Samantabhadra* into some form of eternity is because many people haven't had deep training in inquiry or in negation. In some of the conventional religions in the West, everyone believes in an omnipotent God and performs religious duties. And yet their practice does not always include inquiry, letting go, or negation.

Many of the New Age movements also have nothing to do with negation but rather believe in some kind of "thing"—higher consciousness, chakras, etc. So it is really easy for people to turn zhi into something eternal.

Neurologically we are wired to believe, reify, and put reality into pigeonholes so that it makes sense. It seems crazy to let go of the whole matrix of reality. It is challenging, confusing, and disorienting to our poor brain. But here, we are asked to let go of the propensity of the brain, to let go of an evolutionary habit. We are not being asked to drop a small habit like nail-biting. The tendency to reify things is a huge evolutionary habit in our DNA, in our genes. The Dzogchen tradition is asking people to drop this deeply rooted neurological habit and go into another state of consciousness to experience reality with a new vision, a new perception, where language no longer applies, where intellect is not useful, where words are not necessary, where everything you believe to be true starts collapsing and turns out to be just a bunch of stories.

Yet it is possible to do it. Dzogchen is inviting us to experience zhi, which is not a theory. One can experience zhi through meditation. Dzogchen uses meditation and pointing-out instructions so we can step back from the old brain to experience a reality that has no limitation, no reference point, no duality between self and other. A reality that has nothing to achieve, nothing to purify, and that has no past and no future.

Then this verse says that such reality, this ground, is "a space of deep, profound clarity." Zhi is not nothingness but full of potential, the capacity for zhi nang to manifest. As we said earlier, the metaphor for the manifestation of zhi is called the youthful vase body, which breaks open and reveals the light. This is a wonderful metaphor, because once you think of it in the context of zhi, naturally zhi is no longer nothingness. The verse already describes zhi as ineffable but not nonexistent. It is the great space in which there is full potential for manifestation; it is always present there.

Verse 4 - The Pathless Path of Dzogchen

In the unborn, original purity, which is pristine in itself,
The radiance of the spontaneously present unconditioned shines,
Yet not held as something other, the great union of awareness and emptiness.
The understanding of primordial ground culminates through this realization.
May there be no pitfalls concerning the vital points of the path.

The next three verses in this prayer depict the path of Dzogchen. As we've already said, most traditions in Buddhism tend to describe the framework of their own doctrine with the three principles of ground, path, and fruition. Even though the principles are not identical, they are all connected to each other in some way. In Dzogchen, because it is a nondual tradition, the three principles are not different from each other in essence. For example, the great Dzogchen master Lama Mipham also wrote an aspiration prayer that belongs to the same genre as this text we are studying. In the title of Lama Mipham's prayer, there is the phrase "inseparability of ground, path, and fruition," which points out this very notion that Dzogchen is not just any other yana. It is a nondual tradition in which those three things cannot be separated in their essence.

In general Buddhism, the path is the spiritual journey that we take, in which we do all the practices in order to go through the process of karmic purification and cultivate what is called in Sanskrit *sambhara,* virtuous accumulation.

As we said in the commentary on verse 2, there is an enlightened aspect of consciousness, depicted by Samantabhadra, but consciousness got deluded by the power of original unawareness. Out of that delusion, samsara comes into being, which turns out to be quite a painful reality. Then there is an urge to return to the primordial state prior to samsara, a desire for liberation from samsara, a desire for what is called nirvana or *moksha*. That desire becomes a powerful motivation for us to traverse the path or embark on the spiritual journey.

This verse lays out the foundation of the path of Dzogchen. In Dzogchen, the path is defined as the process or journey through which one realizes primordial awareness, which was already described in the context of ground. In other words, the path is the process of awakening to that ground, which is ineffable and beyond all conditions. Every path in the Buddhist tradition has some goal or objective to be actualized. In Dzogchen, the whole purpose of the path is to realize or awaken to what is called the awareness of original purity, *kadag gi rigpa* (W. *ka dag gi rig pa*). That is the ultimate theme of the Dzogchen teachings. The term *rigpa* is perhaps the pivot on which the entire system of Dzogchen revolves. It has many nuances that have to be dealt with carefully. In general, *rigpa* simply means pure awareness. If there is one term that is most essential to Dzogchen, that would be rigpa. Dzogchen teaches that rigpa resides in each of us in this very moment.

The Buddha is Within

Rigpa is considered the dharmakaya Buddha, the formless Buddha, the highest Buddha. This is why often the Dzogchen masters encouraged us not to seek Buddha outside of ourselves. The whole idea that Buddha is within each of us is the message of Tantric Buddhism, but it is especially well developed in Dzogchen. Dzogchen teaches that the genesis of our own samsara is in this one unawareness: not recognizing that Buddha is already within each of us. This is the premise of Dzogchen, yet it can be challenging to those who may not have such an understanding.

One time, I was visiting Malaysia to lead a meditation retreat. One of my friends asked a group of us to pay a visit to a refugee center. I thought it would be so wonderful to visit and show our support, because sometimes it feels our spirituality can be self-indulgent when we don't put kindness and compassion into action. It seemed this would be a good opportunity to practice love and compassion in the world. At the center were many refugees from Myanmar. Some of my friends gave them monetary gifts in red envelopes, which is a tradition in Asia. One of the people was Buddhist, and I wanted to offer him some kind of gift. I felt that the best gift I could offer was moral support. I thought that he might be confused and lost by not having a home, or in despair and not seeing goodness in himself. That was my projection. I joined my hands saying, "Buddha is within you," thinking that would help him to turn inside and find assurance in himself. As a

Tibetan Buddhist, those were the best words I could give him. He was challenged and reacted immediately. He said, "I'm a Theravadin Buddhist." He couldn't take it. It was too radical or could even be perceived as blasphemy, because many Asian Buddhists think that Buddha is outside, and they associate him with Shakyamuni Buddha. To say "Buddha is within you" is radical to them.

But here, Dzogchen points out that the true Buddha is not outside but is already within each of us. That is rigpa, which is present in all of us. Therefore, Dzogchen has the notion that if you can be awakened to the Buddha within, you do not have to struggle too long. You can experience liberation without going through a lot of effort and struggle. You can be enlightened in the very moment of such an awakening, because rigpa is already in you. It's not like you have to go somewhere or be somebody, or do this and that. There is no limitation to the possibility of awakening, because in Dzogchen, enlightenment is awakening to the Buddha in yourself. A famous saying in Dzogchen goes:

> *If you practice Dzogchen in the morning, you will be enlightened in the morning.*
> *If you practice Dzogchen in the evening, you will be enlightened in the evening.*

This is telling us that not only is enlightenment possible for each of us but it can happen right now, in this very moment. This may sound too easy. How does karmic purification take place without engaging in all the spiritual practices to purify one's karma? Yet in such awakening, without even trying to purify your own karma, it is naturally purified. In *The Flight of Garuda*, Shabkar says,

The darkness in an empty house that lasts for a thousand years
Can be dispelled in a single moment by a lamp.
Likewise, at the moment of realizing one's own mind is clear light,
All the vices and veils of numerous eons will be purified.

The logic behind this is that both nirvana and samsara are two states of mind. Not only that, samsara itself as well as karma and suffering originate not from outside in the ultimate sense but from inside, from our own consciousness, from not being able to awaken to rigpa within.

Various methods and expressions, or terminology, are employed in order for us to realize this very notion that rigpa is within each of us. For example, *zhi cha sum drel gyi rig pa* (W. *bzhi cha gsum bral gyi rig pa*) is a very interesting concept. It is almost like a mathematical way of understanding rigpa and how it is present in us. *Zhi cha* means four portions, *sum drel* means without three portions. There are different ways of interpreting this concept. Traditionally, the three portions are regarded as the discursive thoughts of past, present, and future. They represent categories that include all the possible kleshas that can arise in our consciousness. The fourth portion is nonconceptual thought.

I also heard another way it can be interpreted: if our consciousness is divided into four portions, three might be the three kleshas—greed, hatred, and ignorance. What remains is awareness, or rigpa. This means if you remove those three kleshas, mind is already pure awareness.

This mathematical equation is pointing out that the fourth dimension is always there. It's not like suddenly when you experience rigpa, it is produced by some cause, as if it was not there in the first place. On the contrary, it is always there, and you can experience it when you relax in the natural state of mind as it is.

The Path in Mahayana and Vajrayana

As we said earlier, various schools of thought in Buddhism have their own version of the path. In general, all Mahayana schools agree with each other that accumulation, or *sambhara,* is the path. There are two sambharas, known as *jnana sambhara* and *punya sambhara. Jnana* refers to spiritual practices like inquiry and meditation, whereas *punya* refers to virtuous deeds like generosity and helping others.

In general, the path in Mahayana and Vajrayana is quite specific with many details, and involving a lot of effort or methodologies. For example, the Mahayana Sutras say that the bodhisattva spends three eons on the path just to get somewhere, then she finally can breathe a sigh of relief. The path can also be arduous and is not just sitting on a comfortable meditation cushion in a beautiful hermitage enjoying spiritual bliss. The sutras describe the bodhisattva going through a heroic journey to cultivate the two sambharas. Some of the Jataka tales are mind-blowing—a bodhisattva might give away everything he or she owns, or go through physical hardships, sickness, pain, austerities, and courageous acts practicing the six *paramitas.* It sounds heroic but extremely arduous and effortful.

In Vajrayana, the path is not simple either. The Vajrayana practice usually has two stages: a creation stage (Skt. *utpatti-krama*) and a completion stage (Skt. *sampanna-krama*), which are very specific practices designed to purify our internal defilements on mental and somatic, or physical, levels. The two stages of Vajrayana are part of a complex system. One has to study and learn the details, techniques, and systems of *chakras*, *prana*, *bindu*, and the *mandala* of the deities. The two stages involve a lot of practices, visualizations, and mantra recitation. It is a path that sounds rather elaborate.

Yet all the paths have the same goal, which is simple: to transform our consciousness.

The Nine Yanas

Dzogchen describes itself as "yana beyond mind." First, one may need to understand the whole concept of *yana* to know what this phrase means. We introduced this briefly in the introduction, and here we will give more details.

The term *yana* is used mainly in the Mahayana and Tantric Buddhist traditions. It means vehicle. It could refer to the hierarchical capacity of the spiritual mind. It can also refer to the practices that enable one to progress on the spiritual path. Or it can refer to the entire path that takes one through all the stages of awakening, going to higher and higher states of awakening. Each of the yanas has distinct characteristics.

There are a few different systems of yanas. The Tibetan Buddhist tradition postulates two yanas known as Sutrayana and Vajrayana. The Nyingma tradition goes further and divides the two yanas into nine yanas: three in Sutrayana and six in Vajrayana.

Path of Sutrayana

The Sutrayana, or the path that is taught mainly in the sutras, has three yanas, *shravaka-yana*, *pratyekabuddha-yana*, and *bodhisattva-yana*. Out of these three, the first two are called the *hinayana*, or lower vehicle, because the individuals who are on that path are lacking in *bodhichitta*, the awakened heart, the desire to awaken all beings. They are doing all the spiritual practices with one motivation—to become enlightened themselves in order not to suffer any more. But they would not have the heroic motivation to stay in the world as long as all sentient beings exist, in order to help them.

The spiritual development of the first yana is quite rudimentary. *Shravaka* means listener, which is an archetype of a being or person whose heart is not yet big. Their whole spiritual practice is to find liberation for themselves. They may have seen the absolute nature of reality but their insight is not yet fully matured. *Pratyekabuddha* is the next stage, where one goes beyond the shravakas. Perhaps one's awakening becomes more developed.

The third yana is the *bodhisattva-yana*. The bodhisattva is someone who has a huge heart, someone whose very intention for being on the spiritual journey is not to discover inner liberation for his or her self but to help all beings and assist them in finding inner freedom. The bodhisattva's commitment is to stay in the world and to help everybody become enlightened. The bodhisattva path is the essence of Mahayana, or the Great Vehicle. The bodhisattva's awakening to absolute reality is much more developed than the first two, the shravaka and the pratyekabuddha.

One clear image to illustrate the yanas and the demarcation between them is to imagine that the shravakas and pratyekabuddhas are sailing the ocean in a small boat to reach the other shore, the island of treasures—delicious fruits and precious gems—or the island of liberation, which symbolizes nirvana. The boat symbolizes the path, and the sea symbolizes samsara. But they didn't take anyone; they are just sailing by themselves. They are not simply average people—they have all the skills and techniques. They are skilled boaters who started sailing but didn't want to bring anyone along. Perhaps it was a big headache for them. It could take a long time if you invite everyone who wants to come to this island of treasures. There could be a lot of chaos on the way.

So they decide to go ahead on the voyage because they are done with samsara, done with suffering, done with this existence. They want to say goodbye forever to this existence and enter into the state of nirvana. Forever. For them, existence is samsara. For them, to be enlightened means to be done with existence. Both shravakas and pratyekabuddhas are exhausted with existence. They see life as intrinsically miserable and flawed, and they want to be done. They want to go someplace where they never have to come back.

In some sense, this motive is not unusual. In general, we human beings have this motive, whether we say it out loud or keep it to ourselves. It is a universal desire. Some part of us is not so crazy about existence, even though we are afraid of death and nonexistence. This is pointed out by the Greek philosopher Theognis of Megara, who wrote,

The best for men is to not have been born
and to have seen the light of the sun;
But if once born, to pass through the gates of death
as speedily as may be.

The shravakas and pratyekabuddhas want to get out as quickly as possible. Their calculation is that if they don't have to bring anyone else along, they will get out quickly.

In the Mahayana tradition, samsara is a state of mind. You can still be in existence while being in an enlightened state of mind. The bodhisattva's motive for being on the spiritual path is not from the ego. Its root is in altruism, bodhichitta, the enlightened heart. From bearing witness to the suffering of the world, he or she has the heroic courage to be in the world in order to help others. Not only to be in the world but to keep coming back as long as samsara exists, to help people find nirvana, and to help people with compassion and love. They even help with earthly issues by having an aspiration to feed those who are hungry, heal those who are sick, and protect those who are weak. The true bodhisattva is called an Arya Bodhisattva, exalted bodhisattva—one who is not only driven by a higher aspiration but also has awakened to *mahashunyata*, great emptiness, and sees the world as illusion. Such a bodhisattva is able to keep his or her joy and equanimity. He or she sees the world is an illusion but at the same time is completely compassionate, engaging with the world and doing everything in his or her power to alleviate the suffering of others.

The path of the bodhisattva is not just about having great altruism but also includes practicing the six paramitas of generosity, discipline, patience, diligence, contemplation, and wisdom, which is a deep contemplation on *dharmata,* the nature of reality.

Path of Vajrayana

At some point in their practice, people may want to have a shortcut on the path. The idea of a shortcut is often used to praise the sublime path of Vajrayana and particularly the nondual teachings such as Dzogchen and Mahamudra. In the middle of the path, after all your struggles and effort, if you realize you are not getting to the destination of nirvana, and it seems very far away, it is very natural to have the desire for a shortcut. This is one reason why people have been drawn to the nondual teachings throughout history.

In general, Vajrayana describes its uniqueness by saying it is a shortcut, especially in comparison to Sutrayana, which involves precise stages of enlightenment as well as a lot of time and effort to achieve nirvana. One could compare Vajrayana to Sutrayana with the analogy that Vajrayana is like riding *balaha*, the magical horse, but Sutrayana is like riding an ox. Vajrayana is more advanced than any of the Sutrayana levels. The awakening as a result of Vajrayana is much more developed than the awakening in the first three yanas.

Like the bodhisattva-yana of the Sutrayana, Vajrayana is also based on the principle of bodhichitta. But Vajrayana has a number of attributes that distinguish it from Sutrayana. Vajrayana emphasizes what is called sacred outlook. One not only sees the world as an illusion but also as sacred. Those who practice Vajrayana are not only able to be in the world without a need to reject or escape from it, but they are able to hold the world with a sacred attitude, seeing no fundamental duality between the transcendent and mundane, seeing that it is all sublime and pure.

Vajrayana is about not rejecting. The paths of the shravaka and pratyekabuddha have an element of rejecting life or existence. On the path of the bodhisattva, one doesn't reject life; one sees it as illusion but doesn't yet see it as sacred. There is still a struggle, seeing pure and impure. But in Vajrayana, one not only has the bodhisattva spirit but sees existence as sacred. He or she celebrates existence as a sacred mandala, or sacred world. The path allows individuals not to reject but to enjoy the delights of life and existence without getting caught up in them. One can stay liberated and enjoy life.

One way to understand Vajrayana is through the legend of King Indrabodhi. When King Indrabodhi went to see the Buddha, he asked to be shown the path of liberation. Buddha said, "Become a monk." King Indrabodhi responded that he would not become a monk. He refused to take a path that rejected the enjoyment of life. Then it is said that Buddha taught the path of Vajrayana to the king. This legend tells us that the central principle of Vajrayana separating it from other yanas is that it is not rejecting life but embracing life as sacred. Enjoying life is in harmony with one's path, and rejecting life is an imperfect approach to true nirvana. The *Vajra Dakini Tantra* states,

> *Following precepts of intolerable austerities,*
> *one's body would be emaciated and suffer.*
> *If one's mind is distracted with agony,*
> *the siddhi would go away because of it.*

Another Tantra says,

For many eons,
if one takes on the suffering of austerity,
he or she would not attain nonduality as a fruition.
But it would be accomplished in this life by bliss and joy.

These verses about Vajrayana indicate that it is pointless to torture oneself in the name of enlightenment; it is just not a smart thing to do. The verses hint that you can enjoy all the senses and delights of life, not feel bad about them, and still become enlightened by practicing the Vajrayana path. Sometimes if you try to go against the delights of life, not only will you have unnecessary struggles, you may miss the final point of the path and experience hurdles that prevent you from becoming fully liberated.

In addition to the sacred outlook, Vajrayana has many methods or means of transforming one's consciousness, including deity yoga, mantra recitations, and the two stages of creation and completion yoga. So it is a very detailed and rich system of practice and philosophy.

The awakening of Vajrayana is also not singular. Even in the context of Vajrayana, awakening has its own hierarchy of levels through which it continues to progress. There are always some subtle attachments and things to let go of. These nuances exist because someone who practices Vajrayana can still be attached to various observances, techniques, methodologies, and even theories.

Path of Dzogchen

Then there is Dzogchen. The path of Dzogchen transcends the inferior motivation of hinayana as well as the hardships of the bodhisattva, who takes many eons to become enlightened.

Dzogchen also transcends all the complex methods of Vajrayana. It transcends all of them and goes to the heart of the matter; it is in sync with the truth, primordial ground, original purity, in which there is no path. In that sense, the Dzogchen path can be described as the pathless path.

As we said earlier, the Nyingma tradition developed the system called nine yanas. In addition to the three yanas of Sutrayana, (shravaka, pratyekabuddha, bodhisattva), the Vajrayana has six more: Kriya Tantra, Upa Tantra, Yoga Tantra, Maha Yoga, Anu Yoga, and Ati Yoga. Dzogchen places itself in Ati Yoga, the highest among the yanas.

Dzogchen sees that all other eight yanas are not free from the matrix of the conceptual mind. They all rest on the intrinsic separation between ground, path, and fruition, and they require various methods, effort, discipline, and doctrines as necessary means for awakening according to each system. But the practice of Dzogchen is very simple. There is no complex system. Therefore, Dzogchen regards all the other yanas are being based on mind except itself. *Mind* here refers to conceptual mind, which is the opposite of nondual mind. Nondual mind sees no separation between ground, path, and fruition. They are all one. There is only one reality.

In the end, the focal point of Dzogchen revolves around rigpa, or pure awareness. The path is all about realizing rigpa and learning to stabilize that in one's consciousness, becoming grounded in that realization. Not merely having a moment of such awakening but establishing that awakening in one's consciousness and incorporating it in everyday life.

The Dzogchen path is not completely free from challenges, because even after having an authentic awakening, which could have been brought about by a catalyst such as ngotrod from a master, it is easy to lose such an awakening when encountering external circumstances. Or our old mental habits can simply reclaim us. Then rigpa can be easily obscured. This is why Longchenpa said,

Even though nature of mind is recognized,
without becoming familiar with it, the enemy, conceptual thought,
would overrun you just like a little child in a battlefield.

During ngotrod, sometimes the master will let you know whether you have recognized rigpa or not. With the affirmation of the master, you might feel that you have realized rigpa and want to share that with other people. Such affirmation could be valid in itself. But that does not mean that your recognition of rigpa is a complete, true awakening. If it is a true awakening, according to the system of the stages of awakening, you would have entered the third path, the path of seeing, and be considered an arya, exalted one. So even though the recognition of rigpa has happened, it does not always meet the standard of insight for the third path. Yet it is more than just an intellectual understanding, otherwise you could simply read a lot of books on Dzogchen, accumulate information, and feel that is all you need. So that recognition might be regarded as the provisional path of seeing rather than the *bona fide* path of seeing. This distinction solves a lot of philosophical problems. Because even though that recognition might not be a true awakening, it is a much more profound experience than merely an intellectual understanding of rigpa.

"In the unborn, original purity, which is pristine in itself..."

This verse illuminates the idiosyncrasies of rigpa, or awareness. The very essence of rigpa has nothing to do with any conditions that we can imagine. Therefore, it has never been born and will never die. If something is born, it has to die, which makes it part of the conditioned. As you know, Buddhism has two categories: conditioned and unconditioned. Anything conditioned is part of samsara, and anything unconditioned belongs to nirvana or absolute truth.

But again, the notion that it is unborn does not indicate it is some kind of eternity. It is also not some kind of thing. It is free from all conditions. Its essence is already freed from kleshas and *vasanas*, which are considered incidental obscurations or adventitious. If we think of rigpa like the pure sky, kleshas are like the clouds, which are not the sky. They can obscure the sky but can drift away. A traditional metaphor says that kleshas are like dust on a royal mirror. The royal mirror has always been a royal mirror, whether it is covered by dust or not. There is not one single moment when it is not a royal mirror, even when it is veiled. But once the dust is removed, it can reflect an image. In the same way, even when our consciousness is gripped or shrouded in the kleshas or inner poisons, its nature is always rigpa—pure and enlightened.

Remember that rigpa is not an altered state of mind or some kind of exalted state of consciousness. It is simply the nature of consciousness. Rigpa is always described as uncontrived, *ma chu pa* (W. *ma bcos pa*), which means that rigpa is not some holy state of mind that is created intentionally or is an effect of a cause. Rather, it is always present, at times veiled and at other times not veiled.

Meditation Guidance

Longchenpa offers meditation guidance on how to be awakened to rigpa:

> *Do not manipulate, do not manipulate your mind.*
> *Do not grasp, do not grasp at your mind.*
> *The more we manipulate it,*
> *the more pollution will occur.*
> *Contrived mind will obscure the essential meaning.*

This verse is perhaps one of the clearest verses on how to meditate on rigpa right on the spot. I personally use this verse for myself. Now and then, when I am offering guided meditation to a large group, I spontaneously translate this verse to help people meditate. Longchenpa is saying that since rigpa is already the nature of mind, it doesn't have to be created or manufactured. Otherwise it could not be the nature of mind. Therefore, whenever we meditate on rigpa, although it sounds counterintuitive to the ego, we should not try to get to a particular state of mind or manipulate our mind. All meditation techniques often try to manipulate or transcend ordinary experience, or exalt our consciousness to a higher level, to feel bliss, and so forth. There is a motive involved in such meditation. Here Longchenpa says to let go of all the motives and preconceived notions of what you are supposed to be experiencing.

In Longchenpa's meditation instructions, you don't try to manipulate your experiences. Just leave your mind alone as it is. Then whatever experiences arrive, either good or bad, do not grasp at them. They could be some pleasant thoughts or something unpleasant; something wholesome like love, compassion, or joy; or on the other hand, something unwholesome, like confusion or anger. "Do not grasp at them" means do not follow any of them. He is also asking us not to reject them.

Longchenpa is saying that if you try to manipulate your mind because you don't like what you are experiencing or have a preconceived notion of what you should be experiencing, it's like stirring muddy water. Imagine water in a muddy pond that you want to cleanse. If you pick up a stick and stir it, trying to make the mud go away, the more you stir, the muddier the water gets. Whereas if you just leave the water alone for a while, the mud will settle, and the water will show its true nature, which is clean and pristine. So Longchenpa is saying that when you try to manufacture a spiritual experience, you end up creating more mud, creating another state of samsaric consciousness.

This reminds me of a story. Once while Buddha was traveling, he asked Ananda to go back and pick up water from a canal that they had crossed. Ananda said, "Can we wait? We are approaching a village soon." Buddha replied that he wanted the water from the place they had passed, so Ananda went back. But when he got there, the water was muddy because cows had crossed that canal. Ananda returned and told Buddha he couldn't get any water because it was muddy. Buddha said to Ananda, "Go back again." When Ananda returned to the canal the second time, the water was now clear. The mud had settled. This anecdote has a moral or message that could be interpreted in different ways. One interpretation is that Buddha was telling Ananda that if we leave our mind alone, it becomes pristine.

"The radiance of the spontaneously present unconditioned shines"

Nature of mind itself is freed from all conditions. Because of that, it has no limitations. You can't say it has a size, a shape, or any characteristics. It is not finite; it does not exist in the context of any limitations. At the same time, again, it is not a blank state of consciousness. It is not like nothingness. From rigpa itself, radiance, or *dang* (W. *gdangs*), shines forth.

The verse says its radiance shines without any effort, which fundamentally means it is the natural expression of rigpa. This radiance shining forth refers to the world of phenomena. Liberation comes when you realize all phenomena are natural expressions of rigpa. Everything we are experiencing—our own kleshas, thoughts, feelings, emotions, joy, sorrow, good, bad—and everything we are perceiving is the natural expression of radiance or the display of rigpa itself. If you recognize this as the natural expression or display of rigpa itself and don't perceive it as other than rigpa, then there is awakening, true liberation. This is the awakening of Samantabhadra that we already described.

Yet it is crucial not to just leave this as some grand awakening of primordial Buddha but to embody it in our own experience. In that way, such awakening can be experienced through Dzogchen practice, which would be accompanied by a profound inner liberation. In that extraordinary liberation, our mind is no longer bound by concepts and ideas, and our heart is no longer imprisoned by unhealthy emotions. Such liberation is hard to believe, but it can happen to a human being under any circumstance. True liberation does not only happen when life is smooth—it can happen to us regardless of how difficult the external conditions might be. Throughout history, there have been people who demonstrated such a possibility. Some of them used religion yet others just had common wisdom and figured out how to be free inside. This liberation is not dependent on any kind of religious belief, therefore it is available to anybody. It is simply that our consciousness frees itself from its own self-imposed prison of suffering. Such inner freedom is depicted by the analogy of a snake that coils itself up into a knot, and then it uncoils itself.

Most of our suffering tends to occur while we are enmeshed in the samsaric mind, or the egoic consciousness. In the nature of mind itself, all the mind-produced suffering does not exist. This is not stating that there won't be any struggles in life if you awaken to nature of mind and are able to integrate it into your life. Life does what it does, and it doesn't disappear just because you are a great yogi or meditator. You have no idea what is in store for you or anybody else. Life is unbelievably unpredictable. Illness, accidents, loss, and all sorts of tragedies can happen to anyone. If you have illness, you still may have physical pain even if you are meditating on the nature of mind. However, the reaction that our ego puts on pain, which intensifies and creates another level of suffering, would not be there. The possibility of this unconditional freedom is not even on most people's mental radar. Yet this is perhaps the most wonderful thing that can happen to a human being.

"Yet not held as something other, the great union of awareness and emptiness."

This line is describing the very nature of awakening from the Dzogchen point of view. It is said that true awakening happens by directly experiencing what is called the "union of awareness and emptiness." This turns out to be a ubiquitous term in other Tantric Buddhist systems, which often employ this term along with others, such as union of bliss-emptiness, union of appearance-emptiness, and so forth.

This term is expressing a complete, perfect awakening in which the ultimate truth of emptiness, or dharmadhatu, is no longer some kind of object to be observed or known, and the enlightened mind is the knower. Instead, in such awakening, the duality between knower and known is completely transcended. In other words, in the beginning, there is a stage where dharmadhatu, or emptiness, is the topic to be investigated or understood; and the mind, or intelligence, is the agent that does the investigation. So there is a subtle duality that is not utterly unnatural. But in the end, that duality has to be completely transcended. In the true awakening, awareness realizes that space—which refers to dharmadhatu, or emptiness—and itself are completely inseparable. There is not the slightest separation between what is to be known and the knower.

This is quite an important concept in Dzogchen. This union is pointing out that awareness is the nature of mind, the Buddha within, the dharmakaya mind, but it is not solid, not some kind of thing. It is empty of itself. At the same time that it is aware, it is not totally dead. It is aware with the amazing capacity to shine its expression outward, so we can have this amazing cosmic play of samsara, joy, delusion, and awakening.

"The understanding of primordial ground culminates through this realization. May there be no pitfalls concerning the vital points of the path."

The last lines of this verse make the aspiration that one would be able to realize awareness, or rigpa. Through that, one directly realizes the truth of primordial ground, the ineffable.

The verse also makes an aspiration that one does not fall into the pitfalls on the path. Are there pitfalls on the path? Yes. The answer is that surely there is going to be an array of pitfalls or misunderstandings that one can fall into. One pitfall, for example, is that one could fall into the trap of eternalism or nihilism in relation to ground, rigpa, dharmakaya, the unborn. And there are others.

Ultimately, this verse is reminding us that this path is direct, because what we are seeking is already in each of us. The ultimate truth, one's true nature, one's original face, is already in each of us. It is the nature of the mind. There is no need to search for it anywhere. No need to create anything. With this radical, nondual understanding, simply by resting and relaxing in the uncontrived natural state of your own mind, the most profound awakening will come to you. This is the path of Dzogchen.

VERSE 5 - VIEW, MEDITATION, AND CONDUCT

From the beginning, it is already pure, and the term
"view" does not even exist.
By awareness realizing its own nature, it pulls itself
from the sheath of meditation.
Because there are no reference points, it is freed from the
chains of conduct.
In this womb of the unconditioned nature, naked and
free from conceptual elaborations,
May there be no pitfalls concerning the vital points of
the path.

Traditionally, the path is presented as having three components: *tawa* (W. *lta ba*), *gompa* (W. *sgom pa*), and *chodpa* (W. *spyod pa*), or view, meditation, and conduct, which are the three things one would engage with in order to practice any particular path. Almost all the tenets and systems in Buddhism have their own version of view, meditation, and conduct. They are not always identical with each other, even though they may share some basic similarities. However, Tibetan Buddhism holds the notion that the path is incomplete unless all those three components are brought into the framework. Therefore, there are very rich systems of the path that precisely describe those three parts. Often yogis and monastics might spend a great deal of time learning about these three elements and incorporating them into their spiritual practice.

View, meditation, and conduct are also connected with each other in a symbiotic relationship, influencing each other. The view influences meditation, and meditation influences conduct. However, Dzogchen makes a radical statement. A famous Dzogchen Tantra known as the *Tantra of Self-arising Awareness* says,

> *In Ati Yoga, the Great Completion,*
> *there is no view, no meditation, no conduct.*

This statement is not by any means metaphorical; it is literal. Such statements occur in other systems when they describe the ultimate truth, such as in the *Prajnaparamita Sutras*, where nirvana, samsara, path, attainment, and non-attainment are all transcended. Although some Tibetan Buddhists might be challenged by this statement from the Dzogchen Tantras, they might remember that such transcendence is taught in the *Prajnaparamita Sutras*, which are respected as the words of the Buddha by all the Tibetan Buddhists.

In Dzogchen, transcending the view, meditation, and conduct is not a notion that applies only to the ultimate truth but is applied to the way Dzogchen is practiced. This kind of transcendence is the makeup of everything in Dzogchen—ground, path, and view. When one meditates in Dzogchen, it is done in accordance with this transcendence, which is often simple, direct, and profound.

"From the beginning, it is already pure, and the term 'view' does not even exist."

View, in Tibetan, *tawa*, generally refers to the unique principle or philosophy of any given doctrine, tenet, or sect. Often the views between different traditions may clash with each other. This is why there are philosophical debates between Hindus and Buddhists, and ongoing debates between different sects in Buddhism. Even in the same tradition, there are a lot of philosophical debates and disagreements, which we can easily see when we read philosophical texts. Even today, there are philosophical debates among Buddhists about various fine points of doctrine. Whenever a tradition establishes its view, the tradition automatically feels it has to falsify the other views; their view is their fundamental philosophical assertion, their doctrine about life, and a well-examined narrative about the nature of reality. The view is well-established with a litany of logic and reasoning. It is not just someone telling a story around a campfire. It is "heavy" stuff. Some of the religious views or doctrines may be created by an individual or may be a creation of a collective. But there are always followers who validate the view and defend it at any cost.

But one has to bear in mind that all views come from the conceptual mind. They are mental creations. Since they are all built on the conceptual mind, they always have cracks and faults and often don't capture the vast or the infinite nature of all things. This is why Nagarjuna said he has no views; he has no assertions. He realized that whatever views you come up with have some kind of flaw, because they are all the offspring of the conceptual mind.

For example, the notion of self is a view, and the idea that there is no-self is also a philosophical view. No matter how valid they may appear to the viewer's mind, they are just fundamentally two different mental constructs. There is no "self" and there is no "no-self" in the nature of reality.

Yet everybody is very attached to their view. There's no doubt that some views are closer to the truth or more benevolent, more profound, or more rational than others. But they are all workings of the conceptual mind and have cracks in their system.

Then the question is, what is the view of Dzogchen? On the Dzogchen path, those three components—view, meditation, and conduct—are often mentioned. But what is the view of Dzogchen? Is it another philosophical principle or a philosophical narrative about the nature of reality, about right and wrong? Here, this verse says there is no view. This is a radical statement that could challenge our mind. The view of Dzogchen is that there is no view.

The verse says something even more radical. Not only does Dzogchen transcend the view, but the term *view* does not even exist. This is a direct and obvious statement that the Dzogchen view is freedom from all views. In the realm of the nature of reality, there is not even a duality between what is to be understood and the mind that understands. *View* means there is something for the mind to understand, like self, no-self, and so forth. But this verse says that in the realm of pure ground—the nature of reality that is not touched by our thinking mind, our conceptual mind—there is nothing to view, nothing to see, nothing to contemplate, and nothing to be understood. There is not even a single thing in that realm that our mind can look at, comprehend, and chew on.

"Already pure" means free from everything; *dag pa* or *pure* means freed. There is not any "thing" there. It is freed from all the traps of conceptual elaborations of this and that, "this is it, this is not it," and so forth. It is freed from all of them. From that point of view, there is no view. That is the logic.

View often implies some kind of understanding that is built upon words and concepts. Whereas here, the nature of reality, whether it is called rigpa, or great emptiness, or dharmadhatu, transcends any limitation that we can imagine, such as time, place, and particular characteristics. It is intrinsically ineffable, where duality does not exist even in the slightest way. For example, there is not dharmadhatu to be understood as an object and a mind to understand it. The idea of view is transcended on the Dzogchen path, because a view cannot capture the ineffable. This point is also prevalent in many Mahayana writings.

As Shantideva said in chapter 9, verse 2 of *Bodhicharyavatara, The Way of the Bodhisattva,*

> *The ultimate truth is not in the domain of the mind.*
> *The mind itself is regarded as the relative truth.*

This does not mean that if one is practicing Dzogchen, one cannot use the term *view*. Ironically the path is built on view, meditation, and conduct even though they are all transcended in the ultimate sense. Of course, when we say that the Dzogchen view is no view, it could drive our thinking mind crazy, because it feels so paradoxical. At some point, one has to know how to drop the thinking mind to have a direct experiential awakening to the nature of reality, or to experience true rigpa.

Years ago, I was invited to participate in a friend's wedding ceremony that was to be held in Northern California. At that time, GPS was very new, but the person who gave me a ride said, "Don't worry, the GPS will get us there." So he and I "hit the road," or in this case, the highway. It was fun, and the GPS was telling us where to go. It felt like a magical, omniscient, omnipresent object, something out of the ordinary. Eventually the GPS directed us to take an exit, and we suddenly started driving on small roads into the mountains. The GPS couldn't direct us anymore, and we got lost. I thought to myself that the GPS is like the thinking mind. At some point, you have to take a leap into the unknown. You have to jump off the ledge of the thinking mind. You have to jump off the ledge of the known and leap into the unknown. The mind can take you to a certain point but then, like the GPS, it doesn't work. Then you have to let go of it and use something else.

It sounds contradictory—you have to establish the view, yet the view is "no view." In many tenets, the way to establish the view or doctrine is by relying on scriptures as well as through inquiry. In that context, *view* means understanding the nature of reality according to any given tenet. Some Tibetan masters even talk about completing or finishing the analysis of the view. The idea is that one engages with a lengthy inquiry and analysis using logic and reasoning until one comes to the ultimate conclusion about the true view. But there is no conceptual conclusion as far as the Dzogchen view is concerned. Every conclusion turns out to be just a concept.

"By awareness realizing its own nature, it pulls itself from the sheath of meditation."

Meditation, or *gompa* in Tibetan, is the second of the three principles on the path. It is basically a way for one to go beyond conceptual understanding in order to have an experience, whether of love, compassion, or no-self. In other words, meditation is when one brings something into experience rather than leaving it as a conceptual understanding. Let's use compassion as an example. Our mind can easily absorb a lot of theoretical information about compassion but not yet feel compassionate. Meditation in this context is going further from the intellectual understanding to really feel compassion, to bring that compassion into one's experience.

Forms of meditation are numerous. If you look into the yanas, each yana has its own system of meditation. Often meditation can be dualistic in that the meditator is using a method, technique, and effort to alter the state of consciousness. This is often regarded by Dzogchen as contrived meditation, *chö mé gom* (W. *bcos ma'i sgom*). It has the connotation that we are trying to add or subtract something from the pure, natural state of our mind or consciousness. Whereas in general, meditation in Dzogchen is regarded as uncontrived, *ma cho pa*, (W. *ma bcos pa*), effortless, nondual.

This verse is not saying that all contrived meditation is obsolete along the path. That's not the point. There are times in the life of a meditator or during the spiritual journey where the systems of contrived meditation could be beneficial. But this verse is saying that's not what meditation is on the path of Dzogchen. It's not about exerting effort and using all kinds of methods to catapult your ordinary mind into the exalted realm of samadhi or transcendence. Instead, it is almost like non-meditation, which is, of course, paradoxical. It indicates that in order to experience rigpa, pure awareness, the mind has to be freed from that whole way of meditating. Meditation in Dzogchen has to be totally different from the experience of contrived meditation. It insinuates that such meditation is a form of bondage, an obstacle to the experience of pure awareness, rigpa. In that sense, therefore, true meditation is no longer meditation. It is letting go of every idea of meditation and meditator, letting go of the whole game completely.

The verse says, "It pulls itself from the sheath of meditation." Imagine metaphorically someone takes out a samurai sword made by the best swordsman in the region. The sword would not be seen as long as it is kept in the sheath. When you look at the sheath, no matter how fancy it is, you won't have the sense of a powerful sharp sword. The sword itself that he pulls out from the sheath is perfect—gorgeous, sharp, and reflects the light. When it comes out, you can say, "It's such a powerful sword." It's a dynamic experience; it's an "Aha" moment. It takes one to the edge of seeing the power of the sword. The blade is not decorated, just plain. If it were covered by anything, it wouldn't be a good sword. It is simple, pure, pristine. The sheath represents all the techniques and some of the experiences that are produced artificially during meditation. It refers to any meditation that is based on a reference point. The sword is rigpa itself, pure awareness.

That's what this verse is saying. Rigpa is not an effect of any cause or means of manipulation. When the mind is no longer bound by anything, neither meditation nor grasping and rejecting experiences, when the mind is freed from all its effort, then awareness sees its own nature, pure, pristine, luminous, free, and spacious. One experiences that as the reality.

Uncontrived Meditation

Some Buddhist masters criticized such an uncontrived form of meditation. Their argument might be that such meditation is lacking in any kind of authenticity and would not take us anywhere; that it is simply being lost in some mindless state of mind. But uncontrived meditation is not like meditation in the way we normally understand it. The truth is that it turns out to be the ultimate or highest form of meditation, one that can immediately allow someone to experience the nature of reality, or the egoless state of consciousness, or the absolute. Some scholars also have the idea that this kind of meditation doesn't have good grounding in an authentic tradition. However, it is what Buddha as well as many authoritative Buddhist masters taught. In the *Prajnaparamita Sutras*, Buddha taught uncontrived meditation as the ultimate form of meditation. For example, the *Prajnaparamita Sutra* says, "The meditation on Prajnaparamita is not to meditate on anything." In the same way, Nagarjuna said,

> *Do not comprehend in any way; do not think in any particular way.*
> *Do not manipulate your mind, and relax in its natural state.*
> *The uncontrived state is the precious treasury of the unborn.*
> *It is the path travelled by the Buddhas of the three times.*

He is saying, "don't do anything." These two quotations are just examples, but there are endless others we can take from the sutras as well as writings from authoritative Indian panditas to establish that uncontrived meditation is authentic and has solid roots in the early Buddhist teachings, all the way to the words of Buddha himself.

There is a type of meditation that is an inquiry, where you intentionally analyze and come to some kind of conclusion as wisdom or insight. But in the pure meditation on rigpa, even if you are meditating on emptiness, you don't have to constantly remind yourself, "I am meditating on emptiness. There is no self. It is empty…" Pure meditation is not to comprehend anything. Just by relaxing in awareness, automatically you are experiencing dharmakaya, or rigpa, whereas in some meditations, you have to deliberately conceptualize that you are meditating on no-self, asserting in your mind, "there is no self." In these meditations, there is something to hook onto, whereas in Dzogchen, there is nothing to hook onto.

There are verses in the Dzogchen writings that perfectly encapsulate Dzogchen meditation. One such perfect verse is the pith teaching given by Shri Singha to Padmasambhava. This verse is found in the life story of Padmasambhava. It is said that when Padmasambhava went to study with Shri Singha, during the pointing-out instruction, ngotrod, Shri Singha said:

Whatever arises, do not grasp at it. Whatever arises, do not grasp at it.
Not arising, not arising. Arising, arising. Arising and not arising.

It sounds very simple but it describes what uncontrived meditation is about. While meditating, whatever arises—thoughts, sounds, moods, bliss, pain—do not get attached to any of them. That's what this verse is talking about. Then it invites us to just relax in the uncontrived, natural state of mind. There are times where things are not arising either. Don't get attached to any feelings, thoughts, and emotions, and also don't get attached to the experience of having a quiet mind when not so much is happening.

The idea is that if one doesn't do anything—does not try to create a special state of mind, does not try to get something—and just lets the mind relax in the natural state, that is all that is required. No need to analyze; no need to reject one's experiences, hold onto them, or manipulate them. Once all the mind's tricks are gone, then rigpa or awareness is just revealed by itself.

"Because there are no reference points, it is freed from the chains of conduct."

View is like the basis of the three components, and meditation is the practice that brings the view into experience. Conduct, or *chodpa* in Tibetan, means that you integrate the experience into everyday life. As we said earlier, for example, if you meditate on compassion, at first compassion is theoretical. Then you meditate on it and experience it. Conduct is when you walk away from the meditation session and incorporate that experience of compassion (or whatever you are meditating on) into everyday life.

So conduct is the practice of incorporating the experience of meditation and the wisdom of the view into life, especially into action in relationship to the world. Each Buddhist system has its own way of defining conduct. Usually in other systems, conduct is related to the whole idea of right and wrong: do that, and don't do this. Rejecting and cultivating; actions that are to be abandoned or abstained from, and good conduct or actions that are intentionally cultivated in everyday life. This comes with very strong notions of right and wrong, or skillful and not skillful.

But Dzogchen transcends even conduct. It has no rigid idea of what to do and what not to do, such as, "I should do this, I should not do this." Usually, we are directing our actions, even on the spiritual path, with a lot of concepts and ideas. Here we transcend the idea of directing our conduct. We let go of the whole system and live from pure awareness. The idea is that everything you do would be quite benevolent when you are acting from pure awareness.

This is not like giving a green light so that we can do whatever we want to do. But it is to live our life without a mental state that dictates, "I should do this, I should not do that." This verse says to drop that little voice, the inner dictator. Drop the whole paradigm, and live freely and spontaneously from pure awareness. If you live from that place, your mind is no longer ruled by your ego, thoughts, and emotions. There is freedom and joy without fear, and you will naturally exude your inherent goodness. Your actions will be nonviolent and altruistic, and noble conduct will be a natural expression of that inner state of mind.

In essence, the conduct of Dzogchen is no conduct, which is paradoxical. It is saying that conduct is not just transcended in the realm of the ultimate truth. It is about not being caught up in a lot of concepts about conduct that might be held in other systems. Dzogchen conduct is all about being liberated on the spot wherever you are. Being liberated is not abstract. It means that your consciousness is freed from whatever it perceives in any given moment.

Experiencing the Nature of Mind

The whole goal of Dzogchen practice is to remove all the inner veils and to experience direct awakening to the nature of mind. The nature of mind is always present; it is always there. It's not like you have to go through a whole process and set of techniques, or means of purification, and then once your consciousness is pure enough, you would have a chance to experience the nature of mind. Instead, you can actually stumble over this amazing moment in which you already experience nature of mind.

Nature of mind is a state of your consciousness where external conditions cannot throw you off balance. One will be grounded in the center of one's being when challenges arise in life. You will be able to feel that this existence is amazing, unbelievably beautiful, and exquisite. It may sound lofty, but there are many moments after meditating, sitting in silence, and relaxing into your body when you can feel life is an indescribable dance of something bigger than your ego. This feeling is not based on stories or reasons. You just feel how exquisite this existence is intrinsically. Even though no wonderful stories are happening, simply being relaxed in your body, enjoying the silence, you experience a new opening in your consciousness in which life becomes magical. Perhaps not so much is happening; perhaps a table is nearby, a cup of tea on it. But if you are in the right state of mind, life is intrinsically beautiful. It is full of magic. This is what life is.

So nature of mind is a state of consciousness that is not bound by our habits, our thoughts, our emotional patterns, and all our subconscious tendencies. Nature of mind is the depth of our consciousness, pure, already liberated, already here, already present within each of us.

Verse 6 - Avoiding Pitfalls on the Path

Not falling into the partiality of good and bad thoughts,
And not wandering in an undifferentiated state,
Within the limitless vast expanse, whatever arises is liberated.
By understanding the nature of reality in which all accepting and rejecting are intrinsically exhausted,
May there be no pitfalls concerning the vital points of the path.

There is, in general, a fundamental distinction between wholesome and unwholesome thoughts and experiences. This is why many forms of meditation are based on this very parameter, and one makes an effort to reject non-virtuous or unwholesome experiences and tries to intentionally cultivate thoughts or states of mind that are regarded as wholesome or virtuous. In general, as human beings, we have some kind of basic understanding about what is good or bad. For example, most people would say that certain thoughts or emotions such as jealousy and so on are not good. Such beliefs could come from our upbringing, which is directly or indirectly influenced by our culture or our religion. All religious traditions usually have a very strong moral system that defines what is wholesome and what is unwholesome. Almost every culture also has its own value system where some thoughts and emotions are regarded as not noble or even bad, and some are regarded as good or something to cultivate.

Of course, there is a demarcation between wholesome and unwholesome. Dzogchen is not completely throwing away these value systems. Sometimes we do have to cultivate good thoughts, such as in the practice of loving-kindness. But in pure Dzogchen meditation, we are not supposed to cultivate anything. Dzogchen is stating that these value systems do not represent the ultimate truth, because all these systems are basically mental constructs.

"Within the limitless vast expanse, whatever arises is liberated."

This verse is inviting us to be in union with the state of ultimate truth in all situations, a state that is free from all concepts and ideas of right and wrong. In Dzogchen meditation, one is supposed to open one's mind and heart to all phenomena, both the display of the outer world—colors, sounds, sights, patterns—and the inner world of thoughts, moods, feelings, and physical sensations. One does not try to manipulate one's experience in order to only be in a virtuous state of mind and reject the state of mind that is regarded as non-virtuous. Instead, you welcome all thoughts and emotions into your awareness. You do not label them or judge them but let them all flow through you. Through that, you become pure awareness, which is already free, already liberated. One can even experience what is called *shar drol* (W. *shar grol*), which means whatever arises is liberated as it arises.

When one is abiding or grounded in such awareness, whatever arises doesn't really matter. It doesn't matter whether it is a wholesome or unwholesome thought. Nothing binds awareness, because awareness is not attached to anything. Dzogchen masters often use the analogy of dark clouds and white clouds that equally obscure the sun. A golden chain and an iron chain can equally bind one's hands. The golden chain can be used as an analogy for positive spiritual experiences, and the iron chain is an analogy for ordinary or unwholesome experiences. According to Dzogchen, if you are attached to any of them, your mind is already bound. Even attachment to positive experiences can bind you and keep you from experiencing such pure awareness.

So the actual Dzogchen practice is that whatever might arise—positive, negative, or undifferentiated experiences, (neither positive nor negative)—one should not grasp at it by judging it or thinking, "This is good. I'm going to cultivate it," or "This is bad and I'm going to reject it." One realizes that the whole effort to cultivate and reject is just part of the ego and does not exist in the realm of primordial ground or the nature of reality.

An Undifferentiated State

It's easy to recognize when wholesome or unwholesome thoughts arise. When you have the thought to practice generosity, for example, you can easily recognize you are having a wholesome thought, a noble thought, whether you are religious or not. Unwholesome thoughts can also easily be recognized. If a thought such as jealousy arises, even if you are not a religious person, you can recognize that what you are experiencing is not something noble or something to be proud of. However, the undifferentiated state is the state of mind where you cannot really describe what you are experiencing as virtuous or non-virtuous, good or bad. These states of mind happen all the time. It's not like we are always angry or always experiencing love. A lot of states of mind cannot be put into any category. In every moment, many experiences are those of an undifferentiated state.

The undifferentiated state turns out to be very tricky on the Dzogchen path, because meditators tend to mistake this state as awareness, or buddha mind. The undifferentiated state may sound like true awareness, because not many strong thoughts or emotions are happening. For example, anger or jealousy is not happening. If you are meditating and fall into this state, you may feel it is the dharmakaya mind, or pure awareness, because there is not so much mental activity. If you meditate and follow the meditation guidance about letting go, "don't do anything, relax, do not analyze," then you can fall into this undifferentiated state and think that is true awareness.

Dzogchen masters say this is an area where one should be cautious. It is a very big pitfall on the path. In Dzogchen, this state is called "being lost in *alaya*." Alaya is the state of mind that is lacking in awareness and wisdom, and it has the quality of being almost unconscious and undifferentiated. Yet it is still part of the samsaric consciousness, the unenlightened consciousness.

These mistakes or pitfalls can be clarified and avoided. This is why Dzogchen offers what is called *shen jed* (W. *shan 'byed*), distinction. *Shen jed* is taught mainly to help understand the demarcation between awareness and the state of mind that is in juxtaposition to awareness or could be easily mistaken as awareness. Quite a few distinctions are mentioned in the Dzogchen texts. The most important one is the distinction between dharmakaya mind and alaya.

This may sound a little bit too esoteric. Just hearing the words *alaya* and *dharmakaya* may intimidate you, and you may think, "If I am practicing Dzogchen, I should learn the meaning of them, otherwise I am wasting time." There is a simple way to explain the demarcation. Sometimes when we meditate, we zone out, and not many thoughts are happening. You may be meditating for forty-five minutes or a whole day. You have told all your friends you are not available. Your email auto-responder says, "I am doing a Dzogchen retreat for the next two weeks, and if it is an emergency, here's who to contact." But what you are doing is just zoning out. Your whole brain becomes very slow, and your whole system relaxes, because the world is not invading you. But there is not so much awareness, and this can be regarded as similar to alaya. You are zoning out. Whereas the real meditation has an intelligence, an awareness that comes with so much insight, so much wisdom. It has the power to undo the conglomeration of your karmic patterns. Even energetically, all your channels open, and creativity and love arise naturally. That can be called the dharmakaya mind. So don't zone out when you are meditating, and remember to be fully present. Then you already know the essential demarcation.

Calm Abiding, Clear Seeing

In general, there are two all-encompassing categories into which all meditation practices can fall. This is true for the Dzogchen system as well. These are known as *shamata* and *vipashyana*. Shamata is calm abiding, and vipashyana is direct seeing. Sometimes they are separated as different meditation practices, and at other times they can be infused with each other. In Dzogchen, rigpa is the union of calm abiding and direct seeing. Rigpa is a state of mind that is calm and still. But it is not just that—it has the quality of vipashyana, direct seeing, or prajna, insight, which is the direct awakening to the true nature of reality, or the nature of one's own mind. That direct seeing of the true nature of all things has the potency to bring about absolute liberation, which no favorable physical conditions can produce.

But the interpretation of vipashyana in other systems differs from that of Dzogchen. With direct seeing, the question is, "What is to be seen?" In other systems, seeing is realizing that all things are impermanent, *anitya* in Sanskrit, or *anicca* in Pali; or seeing all things are in the realm of no-self, *anatman*. But in Dzogchen, what is to be seen is the nature of mind that is unborn, free from all the kleshas, spacious, and limitless. Through that, one also sees the nature of reality, dharmata, the great emptiness.

Therefore, Dzogchen often emphasizes that we should not just fall into some quiet state of mind, because then regardless of how long you practice meditation, vipashyana (prajna, or insight) would not take place. Such meditation would be comfortable and may be beneficial, but it would not bring about the ultimate liberation, moksha, or nirvana. This is the attitude held in the Dzogchen tradition. Some Dzogchen masters are very emphatic about this issue. They want to make sure the meditator understands awareness in the Dzogchen context. Patrul Rinpoche, the great Dzogchen master from the twentieth century, writes in a way that is considered not only poetic but also clear and understandable. In his writing, he indicated that if true understanding of rigpa is lacking, either because the master didn't teach it correctly or the student didn't understand it, then someone could meditate for many years, even seventy years, and not get anywhere. Of course, Patrul Rinpoche is known for being satirical, critical, and direct, but we do need this kind of teacher who truthfully and boldly points out the pitfalls that can easily happen on the path. I don't know if there are actually people who never got anywhere after meditating for seventy years, but he is trying to shock us, to wake us up so that we meditate with the right understanding and our effort is fruitful. Once you hear this kind of statement, you might get scared and wonder, "Am I one of them?" And you will stop dozing off while meditating! Patrul Rinpoche sometimes uses these extreme words not out of sarcasm but out of kindness, to make sure that we all get it and become enlightened from our practice. If we are lost in these states of mind without insight, we could be wasting a lot of time even while we tell ourselves that we are practicing Dharma or Dzogchen and think we are getting somewhere.

It is said that when one is practicing Dzogchen correctly, intelligence, wisdom, and compassion emerge from within. In the Dzogchen tradition, there is a process called *tog bul* (W. *rtogs 'bul*). *Tog* is your realization; *bul* means to report, and tog bul is where you report your experience to your master to check whether you are practicing correctly. Often, the Dzogchen masters will welcome your *tog bul* and tell you whether you are practicing correctly or incorrectly. Other Dzogchen masters will say that as long as you are naturally drawn to the wholesome states of mind and action, and your consciousness is permeated with compassion, then you are on the right track, and there is no need to report anything. There is no question to be asked, and there is no doubt to be solved.

One important aspect of the Dzogchen practice of awareness is that it divides meditation experience into two aspects called *né cha* (W. *gnas cha*), stability, and *sel cha* (W. *gsal cha*), clarity. *Né cha* means the state or aspect of the meditation experience that is calm, relaxed, and still. *Sel cha*, or clarity, describes the state of meditation where awareness is fully present. It is open to all the sense impressions from outside and all experiences from inside. It is a wide-open, spacious awareness where all experiences are welcomed. It is not some single-pointed concentration on an object where you shut down all sensory experiences. This is why sometimes Dzogchen teachers encourage people to open their eyes while meditating. It's not about having your eyes extra-wide open but rather not to enter single-pointed concentration. It is to open your senses and welcome the whole world of phenomena. This is very much emphasized in Dzogchen meditation. A lot of meditation traditions have *né cha*, but Dzogchen emphasizes *sel cha* so that you won't go into a manufactured state of mind like single-pointed meditation where the senses are shut down. In Dzogchen, all the techniques are left behind except to leave your awareness wide open.

"May there be no pitfalls concerning the vital points of the path."

This verse is also setting the aspiration not to fall into the pitfalls on the path. There is a whole list of pitfalls described in the Dzogchen teachings. In the context of this verse, the pitfalls are attachment to *nyam* (W. *nyams*), or meditative experiences. Often it is said that one can be attached to the three nyam that happen during meditation: bliss, *dé* (W. *bde*); clarity, *sel* (W. *gsal*); and no-thought, *mi tog pa* (W. *mi rtog pa*). These three experiences are supposed to be very pleasant and transcendental, like some kind of religious, oceanic experience. These mental states are something meditators are always longing for, because they are so extraordinary and such a contrast to the kinds of mental states that we go through each day.

These three nyam are often described as tricky and deceptive states of mind. It is easy for a meditator to get attached to them or to think "That's it, that's pure awareness," because they appear to be out of the ordinary. During meditation, it's very natural for someone to be enticed by any experience that is not ordinary. Unconsciously, people have the idea that meditation should be some amazing or at least an unusual state of mind that is different from their familiar, daily experience. We have a longing for transcendence, for the abnormal states of consciousness. Because of that, a meditator tries to create an abnormal experience and gets disappointed when what arises is ordinary. Whereas in Dzogchen meditation, rigpa, or awareness, welcomes all experiences, whether ordinary or extramundane, without the slightest grasping to them.

The great masters of Dzogchen often advise us to be mindful and not get attached to these three states. Patrul Rinpoche wrote in his most synthesized text on Dzogchen, *Three Words of Prahevarja*, "Again and again, destroy stillness, bliss, and clarity." When he says destroy them, he doesn't mean to literally destroy them. He means don't try to sustain them. In Patrul Rinpoche's own commentary on this verse, he says one should not be attached to the three nyam—bliss, clarity, and emptiness. Not only that, he says you should use the radical method of exclaiming the *Phat* syllable loudly to abruptly destroy those experiences, in order to make sure you will not get attached to them. They can easily take over your consciousness, which can obscure pure awareness.

But these three nyam can often happen when someone intensively practices Dzogchen meditation. They are not hindrances at all in themselves. It's not that they are intrinsically obstacles that we should avoid. When they arise, it is an indication that you are immersed in meditation and that meditation is having some powerful impact on your consciousness. The experiences can be regarded as a sign that your old mental habits are being challenged, and your consciousness is beginning to crack open. But these three nyam are also quite powerful and enticing.

The first is bliss. This does not refer to the ordinary bliss that we experience from eating delicious food or from sensual pleasure. When there is good weather or when we hear music that we love, we experience bliss. The first nyam is more than that bliss. It is feeling that there is no more suffering in your consciousness. You feel completely free from suffering, from your ordinary human emotions. It is so blissful that you don't want to lose the state. It is said that this bliss or joy is not ordinary joy but is like swimming in the divine sea of transcendence where all human suffering is gone.

Clarity, or *sel wa*, does not only mean that your mind is alert, able to see and hear forms, colors, and sounds. Instead, it is a state of mind that is free from drowsiness and dullness. You feel that your awareness is utterly pristine, clear, and alert. It is like hyper-clarity, an extramundane experience that one does not ordinarily have in daily life.

The third nyam, no-thought, or mi tog pa, does not refer to some state of mind that has no mental activities like being asleep or having fainted. It is the feeling of a sky-like state of mind free from all mental activities.

Jigme Lingpa and other masters said that if you are attached to these experiences, you have totally lost your awareness, and you are no longer in an enlightened state of consciousness. So we are not supposed to be attached even to bliss, which has such a spiritual component. Why shouldn't we get attached? Sooner or later, these states will go away, and in the end, we will be disappointed. Also, the Dzogchen masters are saying that the real spiritual realization and insight is not bliss or other experiences but pure awareness. If one is attached to these tempting experiences, then one is no longer in pure awareness. It is said that your awareness is interrupted by the attachment and has descended into the samsaric mind, the unenlightened mind.

Buddhism identifies three samsaric realms, which are known as the realm of desire, the realm of form, and the realm of formlessness. By being attached to bliss, one's consciousness has descended into the state of consciousness of the realm of desire. By being attached to clarity, one's consciousness has descended into the state of consciousness of the realm of form. By being attached to the state of no-thought, one's consciousness has descended into the state of consciousness of the realm of formlessness.

This whole discussion may lead someone to think that awareness, or rigpa, is something unachievable, because it goes beyond the state of the samsaric mind. This can sometimes lead people to have grand ideas about rigpa, and they may alter their state of mind to experience it.

But the paradox of rigpa is that while it goes beyond the samsaric mind, it is extremely accessible. That's why Dzogchen as well as Mahamudra employ the term *ordinary mind, tha mal gyi shepa* (W. *tha mal gyi she pa*). This term can confuse people who think they are trying to get out of the ordinary mind in order to experience something extraordinary. Yet here, Dzogchen is saying the highest state of meditative consciousness or meditative experience is ordinary. Since rigpa is the nature of mind, one doesn't need to seek it anywhere, or wait for it to happen, or employ any techniques or methodology to experience it. Rigpa is always here, always present. So we are not supposed to do anything other than leave our mind alone as it is right now. Then rigpa can be discovered immediately.

Therefore, the term *ordinary mind* is stating that rigpa is not an altered state of mind. If we simply know how to abide in the natural state of mind right now in this very moment, rigpa reveals itself. When we say *nature of mind,* we mean the mind that you are experiencing right now in this moment. You don't have to do anything with this mind. You don't need to manipulate it, add something to it, subtract anything from it, nor grasp at any experience. Then true awareness reveals itself.

This verse is the last of the three verses on the path of Dzogchen. It expresses the interconnectedness between the three elements of the path: view, meditation, and conduct, (*tawa, gonpa,* and *chodpa*). It could be said that the view is the authentic understanding of rigpa, dharmakaya mind, or nature of mind. Meditation is to experientially realize it. Conduct is to live that realization in everyday life.

Conduct is about truly integrating the wisdom of Dzogchen into all activities, so it doesn't just become some lofty intellectual idea or some pleasant meditative experience. Instead, Dzogchen becomes a living and breathing Dharma. In that sense, conduct is reminding ourselves to live in rigpa in all the activities of life, while eating, lying down, sitting, or going. These four activities are the traditional way to encapsulate all the activities that humans engage with in everyday life. They are, of course, what we are doing every day. There are also nuances in those activities, especially in a modern context, when you are on the phone with someone, driving a car, stuck in traffic, cooking, being with others, being alone, or dealing with co-workers. In all these nitty-gritty activities, you can always remind yourself to stay in rigpa. It is said that the result, the fruition of your practice, can be enhanced faster if you are able to bring awareness into daily life. It is said that maintaining awareness at these times expedites your practice, whereas if awareness is absent, your Dzogchen practice can be quite profound on the meditation cushion but it may not mature.

Therefore view, meditation, and conduct are not separate from each other. The view, meditation, and conduct of Dzogchen can be regarded as nonconceptual; they are not based on concepts and ideas. They transcend any kind of reference point. They are about being in harmony with the nature of reality, which itself is nondual and free from all reference points, all limitations, and even all specific characteristics such as good or bad. Therefore, the whole

Dzogchen path is completely nonconceptual, which can be difficult to understand and is often misunderstood.

Beyond the Thinking Mind

As we mentioned earlier, there have been scholars in Tibetan history who criticized Dzogchen, partly because they couldn't comprehend a Dharma outside of the parameters of the thinking mind. At one point, there was even a movement in Tibet against all these teachings that are nonconceptual or nondual. The leaders of this movement thought that all meditation as well as all views had to have some kind of reference point supported by reasoning, logic, and scriptures. They thought that resting or abiding in nonconceptual awareness was "idiot's meditation," as they called it, and it was lacking in vipashyana or prajna. They did not appreciate the Dzogchen idea that all the good and bad thoughts were like chains that bind us. They thought this was some form of subtle nihilism. They couldn't accept the idea that there was no duality between wholesome and unwholesome thoughts. It was too radical for them. Whereas in Dzogchen meditation, we are encouraged not to get attached to unwholesome or wholesome thoughts and experiences, and we are to treat all of them as simply a display of the mind itself.

In the mind of Dzogchen opponents, vipashyana or prajna is related to the mind having some reference point, either in the context of the view or meditation. For example, they would say that no-self or emptiness is a particular "thing," something that can be defined and is not nonconceptual. They would say that during meditation, the mind has to meditate on no-self or emptiness as a specific reference point, so you should not just relax and rest. Some of them cannot imagine how you could understand anything if there is no reference point. But there are two ways of understanding things. One is through the thinking mind and one is through nonconceptual experience.

Our mind understands most things in everyday life through the thinking mind. Even on the Buddhist path, there is a place for the thinking mind, since Buddhism has both relative and ultimate truth. The relative truth is the domain of the thinking mind, which is the truth of the world of division and separation. It is the reality we live in every day. If I am asked to figure out four plus four, I would say eight. I use the thinking mind in that moment. If I didn't use the thinking mind, I would not come up with the right answer. There is a "me" who is analyzing, figuring out, registering information, and there is an object I am understanding. With the example of numbers, I am the one figuring it out, and "four plus four" is the object that my mind is thinking about. This is how the thinking mind works.

But the way we understand the ultimate truth is not through the usual thinking mind. The ultimate truth is undivided, ineffable, and nondual, so the way we understand it is through nonconceptual awareness, which often happens when we meditate. Not through any kind of meditation but through an effortless meditation, *tsöl mé kyi ting ngé dzin* (W. *rtsol med kyi ting nge 'dzin*) or through mindfulness of dharmata, *chö nyi kyi dren pa* (W. *chos nyid kyi dran pa*).

But those who criticize Dzogchen did not understand the subtlety of Buddhism or the masters they held in high regard, such as Nagarjuna and Atisha. All the Dzogchen opponents in Tibet held Atisha as their hero. They felt that he was the one who restored pure Buddhism. But Atisha's understanding is in harmony with Dzogchen. For example, he said:

Dharmata (nature of reality) is free from all conceptual elaborations.
So let your mind rest in that which is free from conceptual elaborations.

Here, Atisha is actually talking about nonconceptual meditation as well as the view. He is saying the nature of reality is free from everything, free from any kind of mental construct. It is something completely undefinable through words and concepts. Therefore, the true meditation is not about cultivating wholesome thoughts or meditating on a theme such as no-self, but rather letting your mind rest in union with the nature of mind. According to Dzogchen meditation guidance, you don't do anything with your mind. You just let it relax. The moment you do something, you are falling into the trap of mundane or worldly, ordinary meditation. If you let your mind be as it is and just be present, not following or rejecting your thoughts, automatically your mind will be in union with the nature of reality. That union is vipashyana, or prajna, because in that moment, the ultimate truth is realized without duality and without going through the thinking mind.

One of the analogies used in Dzogchen to describe such wisdom is a mute person tasting honey. He or she is dissolved into the sweetness but cannot talk about the experience, because he or she is mute. This is saying that the insight in Dzogchen is nonconceptual. It is not a product of the thinking mind, and when it is realized, you cannot say, "This is what I realized" or "This is what I see."

Prajna is Essential

All the Buddhist schools agree that without prajna or vipashyana, there is no liberation. Shantideva said, "One will be liberated through seeing the truth." Shantideva is basically saying that liberation comes into being when prajna arises in one's consciousness. Without that, liberation will not occur, even if you have gone through karmic purification and your consciousness was transformed. Shantideva is saying that unless the truth is seen, *moksha,* or liberation, is not found. This definition of liberation is quite specific in Buddhism and is not some flowery idea. So all Buddhist schools agree that there is no enlightenment until the truth is seen.

Buddhism often categorizes meditation into either transcendent meditation or mundane, worldly meditation. For example, the four formless meditations are regarded as worldly meditations and cannot liberate you. Even though these meditative absorptions are incredible experiences, such as calmness and so forth, they are lacking in wisdom and will not lead you to awakening. In *The Thirty-seven Verses on the Practice of a Bodhisattva,* Gyalse Thogme Zangpo says:

> *Knowing that vipashyana completely endowed with shamata*
> *can utterly destroy all the kleshas,*
> *practicing meditation going beyond the four formless states*
> *is the practice of a bodhisattva.*

Why is having insight, seeing the truth, essential to inner liberation? The answer is this: Buddhism teaches that the reason we are lost in samsara has its genesis or source in unawareness, which is not seeing the nature of reality and being deluded about the way things are. So the way to attain liberation is not by manufacturing liberation through methods or religious purification but by undoing or dismantling the entire development of samsara all the way back to its genesis.

This is why it is so important to see the truth in Buddhism. Whenever such seeing or insight occurs, liberation happens right there on the spot.

Liberation can happen suddenly in one's consciousness, which is why Shabkar, in his well-known text *The Flight of Garuda*, used a vivid image—in a single moment, the cave that has stood in darkness for millennia is illuminated by a single lamp—to describe how awakening can happen immediately when one sees the nature of reality, or nature of mind, or rigpa.

Shabkar's words can be quite radical. The lamp here refers to awareness, seeing the true nature of reality, prajna. He is also referring to some really unenlightened consciousness filled with all the inner poisons, depicted by a cave facing north over eons of darkness. But in a single moment, liberation happens. How could this happen without going through a lengthy process of spiritual practice and karmic purification? The logic is that liberation happens when the nature of reality is seen. Delusion is the state of not seeing the nature of reality, and when it is seen, delusion is gone. Delusion is the very ground of samsara. When that is gone, samsara begins to fall apart.

As a reminder, unlike other Buddhist systems, whenever Dzogchen and Vajrayana talk about the absolute, they are referring to either nature of mind or nature of reality, which are interchangeable in this system. Whereas Madhyamaka does not put great emphasis or importance on awakening to nature of mind. It is treated the same as the nature of anything—house, tree, or any phenomena. Madhyamaka might say that realizing the emptiness of nature of mind is the same as seeing the nature of a brick and doesn't give it special importance. For example, when you read the writings by Chandrakirti, he talks about negation of *svabhava*, intrinsic nature, but he hardly speaks of nature of mind.

So in the end, the consensus among all the schools in Buddhism is that the truth has to be seen in order to attain liberation. But somehow, in their doctrines, the Tibetan masters have different ideas about the authentic realization of the truth. There is no need to dwell on this philosophical diversity or disagreement. But one of the reasons or motives for objections from the Dzogchen opponents is that they strongly believe that we see the truth through the thinking mind, in the same way we understand things in daily life. This is why they argue that one has to study scriptures for a long time and practice analytical meditation before one can know what the truth is. Some traditions put a great emphasis on the study of scriptures with the warning that meditation without understanding the truth would be a waste of time. The practitioners in those traditions spend years of their training debating the scriptures in order to arrive at some perfect, unmistaken, refined reference point regarding the ultimate truth. Whereas in Dzogchen, the emphasis is on nonconceptual awakening. Even though many Dzogchen masters are very educated or are panditas, the Dzogchen tradition does not demand studying and debating the scriptures for years in order to understand the truth. The awakening in Dzogchen is not the domain of the thinking mind. It is the domain of nonconceptual awareness. Therefore, if one knows how to practice Dzogchen correctly, wisdom or awakening is right around the corner and can happen at any given moment.

No doubt there are lots of pitfalls, and one can easily mistake some pseudo-awakening or spiritual experience as true awakening. This is why the Dzogchen tradition says it is important to have a wise and skillful master, one who can lead the practitioner on the right path and who will make sure the practitioner does not fall into those traps. This verse definitely invites us to be aware that the path is not always straight but can zig-zag quite a lot, and there can be *gol sa* (W. *gol sa*), or pitfalls, misunderstandings that can trap us. This verse invites us to hold the aspiration that we will see the pitfalls, avoid them, and succeed at experiencing true awakening.

VERSE 7 - THE KING OF FRUITIONS

Within the space-like original primordial ground,
Just like clouds dissolve into the sky, the display of ground-awareness dissolves.
The outwardly illuminated mind reverses and goes inward.
Within the state of the youthful vase body endowed with the six qualities,
May I reach the citadel of the king of all fruitions.

This verse begins the exposition on fruition. Fruition is usually the final attainment as a result of practicing the path. The order of ground, path, and fruition is a logical, linear sequence. In general, there cannot be a fruition without practicing the path. For example, nirvana can be regarded as the fruition of a path. *Arhatship* is also a fruition of the path, which is emphasized in general Buddhism. As we mentioned earlier, in the Mahayana tradition, the bodhisattva spends a great deal of time on the path practicing the six paramitas. It is said that she sometimes travels the path for eons, and eventually the bodhisattva achieves the ultimate attainment, buddhahood, as the end of the journey.

This whole idea that the result or fruition is the goal that is to be achieved through the journey, the path, is very logical. We can even apply this logic in all aspects of our life. Almost everything we do has this kind of logic. But Dzogchen transcends the duality between path and fruition. It teaches that in the true fruition there is nothing to achieve and nothing not to achieve. Usually fruition has very dualistic concepts—fruition is something to be attained while the opposite is that it is not attained. But the fruition of Dzogchen is that there is nothing to attain or not attain.

Having said all that, there is still an idea of fruition in Dzogchen. In Dzogchen, fruition has to be understood in conjunction with ground. They are not separate from each other. This is quite different from the idea of arhatship, which is the final attainment of the path taught in some Buddhist traditions.

The notion of fruition can give the impression that there is a fundamental duality between ground, path, and fruition. Fruition can be turned into some kind of thing separate from ground and path that is desirable, and if one works hard on the path, one will get this thing called fruition as a reward. But Dzogchen teaches there is no fruition in the ultimate sense. Fruition is just a name for awakening, when zhi nang, the display of ground, dissolves into ground through the power of such awakening, even though there is no separation between the display of ground and ground.

But then why do we even have to use the word *fruition,* since it is just another concept or illusion? The idea of fruition, even though it is not some kind of thing, is very useful. In the ninth chapter of Shantideva's *Bodhicharyavatara*, a dialog takes place between the realists, those who say everything is real and substantial, and the *Madhyamaka Prasangikas*, who teach that even the fruition that is to be attained is illusion. It is not to be attained anywhere and only exists in our mind. The realist might argue, "Then why do you even have this fruition? Why don't you get rid of the whole thing?" Shantideva said even though the concept of fruition is ignorance, because there is no fruition to be achieved, it has to be kept to alleviate suffering. He is indicating that if there is no fruition, what would inspire people to practice in the first place? It is like a carrot for the donkey. The egoic or thinking mind needs the idea of a fruition, otherwise we might not be inspired to practice at all. So Shantideva says we should not abandon the ignorance of the fruition. He explains that this is not considered ignorance that will bind you to the realm of suffering. This kind of ignorance belongs to the category of ignorance that can be called "ignorance that is not a klesha." Such ignorance is useful and has a benevolent component even though in the end, it too has to be transcended.

Since in Dzogchen, fruition is not something to be attained, then what is the fruition? Fruition is simply that all delusions are exhausted rather than an attainment of something. The *Uttaratantra* says, "Liberation is merely exhaustion of mistakes." "Mistakes" here means delusion. This is indicating that liberation, nirvana, or fruition is not something you can achieve and hold onto. It is just the name for the exhaustion of all your delusions. It can also be referred to as awakening to the true nature of reality that always exists.

"Just like clouds dissolve into the sky, the display of ground-awareness dissolves."

This particular verse is describing the fruition or ultimate enlightenment that is unique to the Dzogchen tradition. Here, fruition is defined as zhi nang, the display of the primordial awareness, dissolving into the primordial ground, "just like clouds dissolve into the sky." All the kleshas, vasanas, and habitual tendencies dissolve into dharmata. Then awareness rests in what is called the "inner-illuminated, subtle wisdom." In order to understand this notion of fruition, it is important to revisit how zhi nang manifests from zhi, or ground, in the first place, and how it dissolves back into ground.

This phenomena of zhi nang manifesting and dissolving sometimes occurs naturally to yogis during Tantric meditation practices as well as during the bardo stages. A similar process happens even during the process of going to sleep. Even though zhi nang disappears during some of the stages in bardo, it does not mean that one's consciousness is liberated. But if one is able to recognize that the phenomena are just the pure display of awareness itself, then when zhi nang dissolves into ground, liberation happens.

One time, I was invited by a family, who didn't seem to have any strong religious identity, to visit a hospital in the San Francisco Bay area. The father of the family was about to die. By my observation, it seemed they couldn't handle any heavy-handed Buddhist doctrines that I might offer prior to some simple prayers. So I told them that I was offering a prayer that their family member would return to the supreme source. I was referring to the ground, but it seemed they all understood what that meant. This indicates to me that these ideas are not just some kind of Buddhist concept, but they hold a universal truth, which we all understand in some part of our consciousness.

"The outwardly illuminated mind reverses and goes inward."

This process of dissolution can also be applied to Buddha Samantabhadra's enlightenment. At that moment, zhi nang, the appearance of all things, dissolves back into primordial ground. That is what is meant by the "outwardly illuminated mind" going inward. In that moment, awareness is no longer shining its radiance outwardly but is absorbed back into itself.

Some Dzogchen masters may use the analogy of a crystal to describe awareness. When the crystal reflects light, rays shine outward, which is like the moment awareness is no longer dormant and shines outward. It is a state in which primordial awareness is called "outwardly illuminated," because it is shining out. This is also what is referred to as "the youthful vase body breaks" and the lamp shines out. At the moment of Buddha Samantabhadra's awakening, instantaneously zhi nang dissolves back into itself, as if light is absorbed back into a crystal (figuratively, not literally or scientifically). The Dzogchen Tantras say when Buddha Samantabhadra becomes awakened, awareness goes back into what they call the womb of precious, spontaneous presence, *lundrup rinpoche bup* (W. *lhun grub rin po che'i sbubs*). This may sound like Buddha Samantabhadra dissolves and becomes nonexistent. But according to the Dzogchen Tantras, Buddha Samantabhadra is beyond birth and death. From that moment on, Buddha Samantabhadra remains as the dharmakaya Buddha and becomes a source of blessings to the world.

Again, one thing we have to keep in our mind is that Buddha Samantabhadra is not some kind of eternal entity or separate being. Buddha Samantabhadra is just a name for the awakening of all of us. This reminder is necessary even though we said it earlier, because the language can sometimes give rise to the false notion that Buddha Samantabhadra is a divine entity. The gender is also very flexible here, otherwise we may end up anthropomorphizing Buddha Samantabhadra as a male buddha. To counter that, Dzogchen often uses female pronouns to describe *Adi-buddha,* or the primordial Buddha, as Samantabhadri, which makes it female. Perhaps we should use "they." This is not just a question of gender or identity. I am trying to make sure that readers will not turn the primordial Buddha into a being with a gender. We all should feel free to swap the gender pronouns between Buddha Samantabhadra and Buddha Samantabhadri. There are also sacred representations of Buddha Samantabhadra and Buddha Samantabhadri in union, which symbolizes the ultimate awakening.

Sometimes the entire notion of awakening is murky, because it can be interpreted in so many ways, especially these days. Generally, many hold the idea that spiritual awakening is an extraordinary freedom, the end of suffering, loosening the grip on ego identity, and so on. All these notions sound great. But awakening is alive, a dynamic state of consciousness that is not lost in the realm of duality. It is fully present, aware, and full of love and compassion.

One of the ways to gauge if awakening is authentic or not is whether there is love or compassion in it. If these two things are missing, then one's awakening is not authentic but just the mind playing a trick on itself. As Longchenpa said in *Resting in the Nature of Mind,*

> *By being trained in that, noble qualities and spiritual*
> *experiences will occur.*
> *Sacred perception and devotion would shine impartially*
> *everywhere.*
> *Love and compassion become ceaseless.*

Similarly, it is also said that when Buddha Samantabhadra is awakened, he or she remains in dharmakaya, and the kayas (enlightened dimensions) and wisdom spontaneously arise to benefit the world. Dharmakaya is described as an enlightened dimension free from all forms, all colors, shapes, and sizes.

The term *kaya* can be confusing to some people. It is often translated as body. In some sense, that is a correct translation. But sometimes this leads people to reify the notion of kaya, so periodically I use the word *dimension* to convey kaya, because kaya is not always a physical form that is familiar to us, like rocks and walls.

One may wonder why the notion of the kayas is used in the context of enlightenment. In Dzogchen, the language used to describe the kayas has a unique flavor that differs from the usual Mahayana language. As we said earlier, in Dzogchen, the kayas have much more to do with the very nature of our mind and the qualities of inner awakening. The term *kaya* helps us realize that enlightenment is not just some state of transcendence but comes with wholesome attributes, such as the inner experience of love and compassion, which manifest outwardly as altruistic deeds.

"Within the state of the youthful vase body endowed with the six qualities..."

The fruition of Dzogchen is also described in terms of the six qualities of Samantabhadra's enlightenment. This verse describes how absolute freedom takes place in Dzogchen by using a very famous term, *khyé chö druk den* (W. *khyad chos drug ldan*), the six qualities. These six qualities are not always listed the same way, and there are variations. While there are different versions of these six qualities, they all reach the same conclusion. They are mentioned in the Dzogchen Tantras and are important terms for understanding the nature of awakening in Dzogchen. The six qualities are sometimes used to describe how the first Buddha, Samantabhadra, becomes enlightened without performing even one single virtuous act or purifying any vice.

The six qualities are:

1. awareness is exalted or elevated from ground,
2. dharmata shining to itself,
3. discrimination,
4. liberation upon discrimination,
5. not arising from other, and
6. remaining in its own natural state.

While this list explains how Samantabhadra becomes enlightened, remember that Samantabhadra is not some individual or some being. Yet the way Samantabhadra becomes enlightened can perfectly explain fruition. This enlightenment is not a result of a long spiritual journey to arrive at an extraordinary fruition. Buddha Samantabhadra is awakened from the beginningless beginning. In general,

Buddha Samantabhadra is a way of describing enlightenment itself.

The first in the list of qualities is that awareness is exalted from ground. As we said in an earlier chapter, primordial ground is neither samsara nor nirvana. It is an undifferentiated state. If ground was nirvana, there would be no possibility of samsara to occur. Therefore ground is not nirvana. And if it were samsara, then no one would be enlightened. Whatever arises from ground would be samsara eternally, which would be a depressing possibility. Ground therefore is indifferent. It is the primordial womb from which anything can emerge—buddhas and sentient beings. But primordial awareness emerged or was elevated from that ground and was no longer dormant in ground. So awareness manifested.

As awareness is elevated or exalted, simultaneously the display of ground also appears and unfolds. So the second point is "dharmata shining to itself." In that moment, even though the display of ground emerges, as if seemingly separate phenomena emerge from ground, or awareness, yet there is not one speck of phenomenon that is separate from awareness itself. Nothing is separate from dharmata, nature of reality, or ground. This is why it is said to be "shining to itself."

Therefore, from the very beginning, there has never been any duality. The duality that our egoic mind often experiences as reality is an illusion. It is like a big dream. Everything is happening within the boundless realm of awareness, dharmata. But it is not happening without consciousness—there is awareness that can witness and experience the display.

By the way, this is not an abstract concept but is something that meditators can experience directly.

So the display of ground is not happening mechanically. There is a place for awareness, consciousness, in this whole paradigm, which is different from reductionist materialism in which consciousness isn't included in the picture. Once somebody told me about a theory answering the question, "Why are we here?" The theory said that the universe is so beautiful, filled with stars, galaxies, and unbelievable magic, but if we were not created, then no one would appreciate it. I like that idea; it is very positive. We need awareness, otherwise this whole creation, which doesn't have a creator, is kind of pointless. So there is awareness, and everything is happening within that awareness. That is the second quality of awakening.

The third quality is discrimination. In that moment of awakening, Buddha Samantabhadra realizes that the display of ground, all phenomena—lights, colors, all forms, no matter how grand or solid they may appear—are all an expression of his own awareness. This recognition happens simultaneously as the appearances arise, without one single moment's gap, without prior inquiry or meditation.

The next quality is "liberation upon discrimination." Even though it sounds like there is an order, liberation does not happen after discrimination. In the same moment, simultaneously, liberation happens. It is not like there is the first moment of time, then the next, and so on. In that moment, Buddha Samantabhadra becomes enlightened, liberated, and never has to wander in samsara for even one single moment.

Often there is a philosophical argument. How can the enlightenment of Buddha Samantabhadra happen without cultivating any kind of *sambhara*, the spiritual virtuous accumulation? In general, accumulating sambhara is like an essential requisite for enlightenment for anyone, regardless of who they are. We explained earlier there are two kinds of sambhara, *punya* and *jnana*, merit and wisdom. The answer from Dzogchen masters to this criticism is that Buddha Samantabhadra completed "the great sambhara of uncontaminated wisdom." This means accumulating wisdom without someone accumulating nor something to be accumulated. The awareness of Samantabhadra is the highest, unconditioned version of sambhara.

The fifth quality is "not arising from other." In that moment of awakening, wisdom simultaneously not only becomes liberated but becomes dharmakaya, the ultimate fruition, the highest attainment. Buddha Samantabhadra arrives at the pinnacle of primordial purity, even though Buddha Samantabhadra was never separate from it. That awakening did not come from other conditions or catalysts. Instead, awareness is awakened to itself on its own. The awakening of Buddha Samantabhadra happened without needing one verse spoken from any one. No one had to help or guide the awakening of Buddha Samantabhadra; there was no need of a master, merit, or catalyst to induce awakening. In that moment, Buddha Samantabhadra is awakened to itself and the nature of reality.

The last quality is "remaining in its own natural state"—that is, remaining in dharmata. Once Buddha Samantabhadra is awakened, Buddha Samantabhadra cannot be deluded, because from then on, Buddha Samantabhadra remains liberated eternally in the realm of dharmata, the state of the nature of reality. But when we use the word *eternally,* it is not in the theistic sense. It means that liberation will never be lost.

A big debate exists among Dzogchen practitioners about this idea that awareness is being liberated. The first question is "where." It's not like Buddha Samantabhadra was born in some Buddhist heaven. So upon what ground, or where is Buddha Samantabhadra liberated? However, the liberation of Buddha Samantabhadra is simply recognizing the display of ground as inseparable from ground itself, and then instantaneously the display of ground dissolves back into ground. So this awakening is not separate from ground. Therefore, Buddha Samantabhadra's awakening is in primordial ground, which is not a physical place.

But then some say that if primordial ground is not nirvana and is undifferentiated, does this mean that Buddha Samantabhadra can fall from that ground? They ask, "Can Buddha Samantabhadra be deluded?" They think that since ground is not nirvana and has the potential for delusion, it is not an absolute assurance to say Buddha Samantabhadra is awakened in ground. To clarify that doubt, instead of saying "liberated in ground," some Dzogchen masters would say "liberated in original purity." Once enlightened in original purity, or *ka dak* (W. *ka dag*), it is impossible for any kind of delusion to arise. However, the truth is that ground and original purity are not two separate things.

Three Qualities

Sometimes Samantabhadra's spontaneous awakening is also described by a set of three qualities: the pith instruction that has not arisen from the scriptures, the enlightenment that has not arisen from mind, and the fruition that has not arisen from a cause.

The first quality means that Buddha Samantabhadra is primordially enlightened and did not need to find a master or get teachings from others. Buddha Samantabhadra did not need any kind of external causes and catalysts for such awakening. Here, the term *scriptures* refers to external teachings or teachers from outside.

The second quality, "enlightenment that has not arisen from mind," means that Buddha Samantabhadra is enlightened because primordial awareness, nature of mind, is already wisdom. That wisdom is self-illuminated or self-awakened, whereas our mind, made of the eight samsaric consciousnesses, is unenlightened. This wisdom of Buddha Samantabhadra does not belong to the eight consciousnesses of samsara (eye consciousness, ear consciousness, and so on, up to alaya consciousness). While our ordinary consciousness has to be purified or transformed to experience awakened mind, the consciousness of Buddha Samantabhadra does not need to be purified. It is already pure, pristine, enlightened. So Buddha Samantabhadra is enlightened simply because primordial wisdom is already enlightenment itself. One could say primordial wisdom is self-enlightened, self-illuminated and self-liberated.

The third quality is "the fruition that has no cause." In general, karmic fruitions have some kind of cause, either wholesome or unwholesome. Even virtuous fruitions often have a cause, whereas Buddha Samantabhadra's enlightenment is not a fruition of any virtuous cause, such as wholesome karma. Buddha Samantabhadra's awakening is the ultimate fruition, *samyaksambuddhahood*, yet it does not come from a cause.

Those three qualities describe how Buddha Samantabhadra is enlightened from the very beginning without having a teacher, entering the path, or practicing good deeds. All these things have been transcended from the very beginning, because Buddha Samantabhadra has never been deluded for a single moment. The nature of primordial wisdom is intrinsically self-liberated.

Once again, the very factor that brings about the awakening of Buddha Samantabhadra, which is clearly described in the Dzogchen Tantras, is prajna, or in Tibetan, *sherab* (W. *shes rab*). In general, across all schools of thought in Buddhism, prajna is the key factor for awakening. But that does not mean that the quality of prajna is identical among all schools of thought. Definitely, prajna in Dzogchen is quite different from the usual insight or prajna that is talked about in various scriptures. In general, insight or wisdom is described as either intellectual or intuitive. But in Dzogchen, prajna should not be regarded as either intellectual or even intuitive. It is difficult to describe. All we can say is that it is nonconceptual wisdom. That is quite safe to say.

In the end, this verse is using unique Dzogchen language to describe enlightenment, nirvana, or fruition. Other systems describe enlightenment with their own unique language. But here, to restate this, enlightenment is the state in which all zhi nang and everything—duality of samsara and nirvana, karma, vasanas, suffering, all our own phenomena—dissolve back into primordial ground through the power of prajna, wisdom. Not only have they dissolved back into primordial ground, but because of the power of prajna, there is fruition of the perfect awakening, the citadel of the king of all fruitions. In other words, the awakening is the state of *samyaksambuddhahood*.

This image of the citadel conveys the image of an awakening that is like a fortress so well-built and fortified that no enemies can attack or destroy it. One can live there happily, enjoying a feast. This kind of awakening experience is not a legend of something that happened to Buddha Samantabhadra as an individual. This experience can happen to someone through the practice of Dzogchen. Sometimes the language may be hard for people to relate to, but as one engages with Dzogchen practice, the language becomes less obtuse and obscure. It becomes very alive.

Verse 8 - Fruition Beyond Effort

To Samantabhadra, the primordial self-aware awareness,
All the notions of attainment dissolve into space.
The nature of Ati Yoga goes beyond effort and mind.
In the expansive womb of Samantabhadri, the union of space and awareness,
May I reach the citadel of the king of all fruitions.

This verse is again describing fruition in Dzogchen. In these verses, fruition is referred to as the "king of all fruitions," indicating in Dzogchen, it surpasses or goes beyond the notion of fruition held in other philosophical systems, which often have a linear order: there is a path, or the Dharma, and by practicing it, eventually some kind of desirable fruition can be obtained. Traditionally, fruition is the result that you will attain from your spiritual practice. It comes with a lot of hopes and aspirations. But Dzogchen transcends a linear, dualistic fruition that is a result of effort. Even though Dzogchen uses the word *fruition*, it does not mean fruition in the usual sense. On the contrary, even the idea of fruition is transcended, because there is nothing to attain.

Not only Dzogchen but also Mahayana to a certain extent transcends the idea of fruition. It transcends attachment to attainment, so there is not even a fruition that you can aspire to. The fruition to be attained is an illusion in the realm of dharmadhatu. This idea is so radical that even many Buddhist thinkers had a difficult time accepting it.

Dharmadhatu

This verse is saying that Samantabhadra, which is primordially enlightened, self-risen awareness, is completely in union with space. Space, in this context, refers to dharmadhatu. In such a realm of awakening, even the idea of attainment is no longer there. The idea of attainment only exists if there is an intrinsic duality between something to be obtained and someone who will obtain it by walking the path. This duality is completely dissolved and never existed in the first place in the realm of dharmadhatu.

Dharmadhatu, or *chos ying* (W. *chos dbyings*) in Tibetan, is one of the most important concepts across all the Vajrayana traditions. The term is employed in the sutras of Mahayana, Vajrayana, and Dzogchen. The word *dharmadhatu* is constructed from two Sanskrit words, *dharma* and *dhatu*. The word *dharma* in Sanskrit sometimes has two meanings. One meaning is Dharma as the path. The other meaning is dharma as all phenomena. In the case of dharmadhatu, *dharma* means everything, all phenomena. The word *dhatu* here means source. So dharmadhatu is the source from which everything arises. It is not a mental construct that someone invented hundreds of years ago, but it is also not something you can point to. It is not a material object nor is it a concept.

You can't figure out what dharmadhatu is, but talking about it invites you to a dimension of reality where your thinking mind is no longer there. You drop the thinking mind along with thoughts, concepts, and ideas even trying to think about what dharmadhatu is. This is an example of one of the techniques in Dzogchen that helps us go beyond the thinking mind and experience a realm of reality that is not completely influenced or constructed by our thinking mind. You can experience a nonconceptual state of consciousness simply by meditating on dharmadhatu in this way.

The definition of dharmadhatu is not static. It refers to primordial ground, nature of mind, emptiness, or *tathagatagarbha*, buddha nature. It can be translated as the realm of all phenomena as well as the true nature of all things. It sometimes can be synonymous with *dharmata*, the true nature of reality. It all depends on the interpretation. Even among Tibetan Buddhist lineages, sometimes the definition differs. In the writings of the Nyingma masters, it seems dharmadhatu is often used as a synonym for emptiness and also for buddha nature.

Therefore, dharmadhatu is a very rich, umbrella-like concept that encompasses the quintessence of the Mahayana Buddhist doctrine. For example, Nagarjuna is known for his exposition on the great emptiness. But he also wrote a hymn to dharmadhatu, *In Praise of Dharmadhatu,* which asserts that the nature of mind is dharmadhatu, already unconditioned, pure, and luminous in itself. This is in harmony with the idea of buddha nature or tathagatagarbha. One of his verses says:

> *If that is not fully understood,*
> *one would be bewildered in the realm of the three existences.*
> *It certainly resides in all beings.*
> *I pay homage to dharmadhatu.*

Here he is stating that dharmadhatu resides in all sentient beings and is the same as nature of mind that is taught in Dzogchen. Dzogchen, and Vajrayana in general, teach that the nature of mind is already enlightened. When one wakes up and realizes the nature of mind completely, one becomes enlightened. An interesting expression in Dzogchen says, "Primordially, it is already enlightened, and once again, it becomes enlightened." This means that the nature of our mind is already enlightened without doing anything, without purification or accumulation of sambhara. This is important because if the nature of mind is not enlightened from the beginning, no one would become enlightened at all. Yet this is saying that when one becomes enlightened, it is as if one becomes enlightened a second time.

This requires some clarification. When Dzogchen or Vajrayana state that the nature of mind is already enlightened, it is not the same enlightenment that is gained through traveling the path of karmic purification and cultivating virtue. It means that the nature of mind, or dharmadhatu, doesn't have any intrinsic flaw; it is not conditioned by karma or delusion. From that point of view, it can be regarded as a kind of primordial enlightenment.

With the understanding that dharmadhatu resides in all of us, enlightenment becomes nothing more than removing the veils in our consciousness that prevent us from seeing the timelessly present dharmadhatu within. Enlightenment is not some kind of attainment but is removing whatever obscures us from seeing the true nature of mind. Once there is no more obscuration and nature of mind is awakened to itself, that state is called dharmakaya or nirvana, as Nagarjuna says in the following verse in his hymn to dharmadhatu:

Whatever is the cause of samsara,
by purifying it,
that state of purification itself is nirvana.
It is dharmakaya as well.

So dharmadhatu can be interpreted as the fundamental ground from which everything arises and everything dissolves, yet itself is always infinite, ineffable, complete, and perfect. Within it, there is no samsara, no path, and there is no fruition to be attained. It is beyond mind, beyond our intellect. No more effort is needed. Usually effort is needed on the path to cultivate sambhara and to purify karma. But within dharmadhatu, none of these are there. There is nothing to be purified and nothing to be obtained.

This is the main philosophical linchpin of Dzogchen as well. In other words, one could say that dharmadhatu is the underlying reality of all things that we are experiencing—sorrow, joy, birth, death, coming, going, being awakened, being deluded. One could say that dharmadhatu is always here, it transcends time, and it is unaffected by anything that is happening in our lives, in our consciousness, or in the world. Dharmadhatu is always present as the basic ground even though it is not some kind of thing. Yet it is not eternity either, since it is not a thing. One of the mistakes that can be made about dharmadhatu is to interpret it as some type of eternity.

This is not abstract either; it is not a mental construct. It should not be postulated as being real or unreal. Yet during meditation, sometimes our mind is much clearer and freed from all its mental veils. Then we can tap directly into this extraordinary and liberating reality. This is why when

Dzogchen masters talk about dharmadhatu, they are not speaking about it as a philosophy but as their experience. For example, when you read works by Longchenpa, he is definitely talking about something he experienced and is so familiar with. It is like a virtuoso talking about her musical instrument. She is a complete expert at playing it.

At the same time, dharmadhatu is not some kind of dead nothingness. In the realm of dharmadhatu, there is pure awareness that has *tsal* (W. *rtsal*), or potential energy, which is the extraordinary capacity or openness from which the whole world of illusion can arise. If that was absent, then dharmadhatu would be a dead philosophical concept in which nothing could happen. We don't know what that would be like, but it doesn't sound good. It would be like some kind of eternal flatness.

Dzogchen often describes the whole world of phenomena as the ornament of dharmadhatu. This is talked about quite often in Longchenpa's famous text, *Dharmadhatu Kosha*, or *Chos Ying Dzod* in Tibetan. In some ways, this idea of phenomena as an ornament of dharmadhatu can be regarded as quite an uplifting and sacred outlook on everything, which is sometimes not found in other Buddhist systems. In the sutras, sometimes there is a perspective on the world and life that is not very uplifting, such as the idea that the whole world is samsara, or everything is just a crazy display of delusion, or a bunch of entangled karmic formations. But Dzogchen is saying that the whole world is an ornament of dharmadhatu.

This is an uplifting tone, which captures the Dzogchen ethos. One could say that the spirit of Dzogchen is uplifting and joyous. This is also expressed in Shabkar's *Flight of the Garuda*, which says:

All things are like the rainbow in the sky and reflections of the moon in the water.
When the yogi realizes this nonduality of appearance and emptiness,
all the phenomena of samsara and nirvana are the show of illusion.
While watching the show of nonduality of appearance and emptiness,
The yogi with unchangeable mind is happy.

Shabkar is also describing the notion of *guyang lobde*, spacious and happy. Here, "yogi" refers to a true Dzogchen master or practitioner who gained unshakeable confidence in this absolute truth. Because of that, such a yogi would not be conflicted or internally disturbed by thoughts and emotions. Whereas many people in the world are very much at the mercy of the continuous, flimsy nature of thoughts and emotions, which often oscillate between joy and sorrow.

In Shabkar's verse, "happy" is not happiness in the ordinary sense. It means that one is grounded in such spiritual realization, and there is deep equanimity; the outer conditions and inner experiences have no more power to throw one off balance. Someone in such a state of equanimity has the emotion of joy. This joy is described by many Tantric Buddhist adepts, such as the Indian Mahasiddha Lavapa, who said:

The deep and vast ocean is filled with gems;
the rulers of the nagas enjoy them. How marvelous it is.
Just like that, all the sights and sounds are primordially dharmakaya.
The one who has such realization enjoys them. How marvelous it is.

This is similar to the language of Dzogchen. He is giving us an image so our mind can touch the experience of this enlightenment. He is inviting us to imagine a great ocean filled with gems where the rulers, the naga spirits, are enjoying the precious gems, and the whole scene is an enchanting marvel. He is using this imagery to express the joy that comes from realizing that everything—sounds, sights, thoughts—are a display of dharmakaya. With that realization, you can experience the whole world of phenomena as a great marvel, some kind of extraordinary wealth, show, or enjoyment.

"All the notions of attainment dissolve into space. The nature of Ati Yoga goes beyond effort and mind."

The ultimate fruition is obtained—even though there is not something to be attained—without a single moment of effort required. This turns out to be a radical proposal because, as we already discussed, all fruition is usually achieved through some kind of complex spiritual effort. One way this notion is expressed in the Dzogchen Tantras is called the "twelve vajra laughters." They are twelve statements that end with the sound of laughter, "Ha! Ha!," symbolizing amazement as well as great bliss from seeing such a reality. In other words, it is like having an "aha" moment with total rapture. Because these twelve vajra laughters are considered radical, there is a warning that people can misunderstand them easily.

Sometimes those twelve vajra laughters are considered ultimate statements that transcend the very notion of cause and effect. This is quite unconventional because, as we know, in Buddhism, samsara, path, and nirvana are usually described in the language of cause and effect. This, of course, makes sense because nothing comes into being without some kind of cause. Everything that exists has a cause, not just in ordinary reality but also in spiritual reality, such as enlightenment. In some sense, enlightenment does not just arise by itself. It is often a fruition of a noble effort. But this is only true in the context of relative truth. In the ultimate truth, even cause and effect are illusions. In the realm of dharmadhatu, no one is there, so no one gets deluded. Who walks the path? Who gets enlightened?

For example, the sixth vajra laughter says:

Oh, Vajra Speech. Look at the essence of the utterly pure,
empty awareness.
How wondrous it is that fruition is discovered in itself
without effort.
By arriving at this single meaning, all samsara and
nirvana are purified within nonduality.
Ha! Ha!

Of course, this is not rejecting fruition or attainment. It is stating that in the realm of dharmadhatu, there is nothing to attain, and there is no one who is going to attain it, because dharmadhatu is the pure, basic, nondual nature of all things. As a being, we will experience the myriad conditions, such as being born, dying, suffering, happiness, attainment, non-attainment, and so forth, that are all part of this illusory drama, or *maya*. Even while the illusory drama is playing out, there is a dimension underlying it that is untouched by what is happening in it. This dimension is the dharmadhatu. But it is intrinsically nonconceptual. We can talk about it, we can conceptualize it, but words and concepts are never going to perfectly capture it. Yet if we direct our mind towards this ineffable, not only does it reveal itself, we can also develop an intimate relationship with it. Then we can live more from that dimension, which allows us to experience the joy of being alive in all conditions.

"In the expansive womb of Samantabhadri, the union of space and awareness, may I reach the citadel of the king of all fruitions."

In Dzogchen, fruition, or enlightenment, is the absolute union of awareness with dharmadhatu. It is sometimes called the union of space (which is dharmadhatu in this case) and awareness. This union is a place where the ultimate freedom, or the citadel of absolute liberation, is discovered. It is referred to here as the "expansive womb of Buddha Samantabhadri." The expanse of the womb gives a clear image or simile of returning to the divine womb, the sacred womb, and becoming completely liberated. Samantabhadri, again, refers to the union of space and awareness, which is the complete awakening where awareness fully realizes space in a nondual fashion; they are not separate from each other.

This union of awareness and space is emphasized as the ultimate goal of all the Tantric Buddhist practices. Such a union is talked about throughout the Tantric Buddhist teachings. One of the Buddhist Mahasiddhas known as Guru Dhokari said:

> *In the natural container of dharmadhatu,*
> *put the ingredients of dharmakaya awareness.*
> *The fruition of nonduality of space and awareness*
> *is realized by the awareness of fortunate yogis.*

Even though awareness and space, or dharmadhatu, have never been separated, our mind requires some imagery to understand their interconnection. Therefore, this verse gives quite a wonderful image of space and awareness. It is inviting us to think that dharmadhatu is like a container, and awareness is some kind of ingredient that goes into it. The image does not mean that they have been separated and we are putting them together. However, the image helps us picture their union.

So the "union of space (dharmadhatu) and awareness" is a state of awakening in which the true realization of the nature of reality occurs. "Union" here refers to the complete understanding, an experiential understanding, in which nonduality is realized. There is no subject and object. There is no difference between dharmadhatu as something to be realized and awareness that realizes it. That whole duality is transcended in such awakening.

This union is expressed again and again throughout Vajrayana teachings as well as through analogies such as the one we just quoted by Dhokari. Longchenpa also uses grand imagery to describe this union. In the second chapter of *Dharmadhatu Kosha,* he describes the absolute truth poetically. He said that in the palace of bodhichitta, the king of self-arisen primordial wisdom resides. The display of *tsal* are his ministers. The true meditation, the nonconceptual meditation, is the queen. His vast kingdom is dharmadhatu. This is again another imaginative illustration to describe the union of dharmadhatu and awareness. This union is the most vital point in the entire Vajrayana. It is just one topic, but it could be described or discussed in a hundred ways.

A Glimpse of the Truth

The idea of dharmadhatu is so vital to the whole Dzogchen system that it should not be treated as some abstract or esoteric concept. One should have a general idea of what it is, if not a full empirical understanding of it. Even though dharmadhatu is not some kind of material object that we can see, in some sense it is not that difficult to glimpse. Some people might be able to glimpse it spontaneously while others may have difficulty feeling that the whole notion resonates or makes sense to them. The factors behind these differences is a great mystery. It may have to do with one's karmic inclination. Often the Dzogchen masters say if you have the right state of mind and readiness, then you don't need to be a great meditator or someone who is well-learned. Dharmadhatu or absolute truth will reveal itself spontaneously, and one will easily be able to glimpse it. If one doesn't have all the right internal conditions, if one is not a vessel for such awakening, then one can engage with doctrines and theories but the realization of dharmadhatu will be far away.

I heard one story about a monk who was an abbot, or *khenpo,* of a monastery in the Kham region. He was well-learned and studied all the Buddhist sutras and tantras. But he felt he never had even a glimpse of the true meaning of

Dzogchen, and he wanted to have an experience of it. He set off to study with the various contemporary Dzogchen masters at that time. Yet even after receiving the profound teachings from them, he felt he didn't get the meaning experientially. On his way back, the khenpo ran into an ordinary lama living in a village and shared his experience. Then the lama said, "I'm not a Dzogchen master, but let's just sit together and pray." Since this lama was not a Dzogchen master, the khenpo didn't have any expectations or resistance. So they sat together and a huge opening happened where he spontaneously understood Dzogchen directly. He had a profound insight. From then on, he realized whatever texts he read or teachings he heard were presenting the same truth.

It is very difficult to say what can wake someone up to the absolute truth. There is not really one way. As you can see, these anecdotes show that such awakening can happen in all sorts of spontaneous situations. But I believe that one of the powerful ways to glimpse the absolute truth is through silence. This may be why the ancient Dzogchen masters wrote complete manuals on how to practice Dzogchen, in which observing silence and doing nothing is often recommended. In silence, with the right intention to wake up, there is a point where one is no longer hooked into mind's phenomena. One begins to see the big reality, one that is bigger than one's thoughts, opinions, beliefs, or concepts; a reality that is also transcendental and not bound by any limitations. This is what silence is for. When we observe silence, naturally there is an awareness that witnesses our own mind, our own mental process. I believe that silence is very important for all spiritual practitioners even though we might be doing different forms of spiritual practice.

Silence is a noble practice observed by Buddha himself. One time, a very powerful and courageous king, King Ajatasattu, wanted to meet with Gautama, the Buddha. He asked his royal physician to take him to see the Buddha. When they arrived at the mango grove where Buddha was residing with his disciples, there was no sound coming from anywhere. It was completely silent. The king got scared and even became paranoid. Because it was so silent, he thought maybe he was being taken to his enemy's place and was going to be trapped. This is one of those anecdotes showing that Buddha observed silence. It is true that Buddha taught the Vinaya, with its many rules, regulations, disciplines, and rituals; and Buddha also taught Vajrayana to a few individuals who were ready. But silence is one of the methods Buddha taught, and he himself observed it again and again.

I have been leading many meditation retreats, and so far I have not called them Dzogchen retreats. Yet my aspiration is that all the participants would have the opportunity to go deep in their meditation and touch the ground—whatever we call it, the dharmadhatu—that is unknown to the usual consciousness. During those retreats, one of the main practices for participants is just to sit in silence and listen to the teachings. I try to bring the Dzogchen voice into my talks, even though they are not labeled as Dzogchen. Many of the meditation retreats may last for a week. The first evening is a ceremony inviting people to hold the right aspiration and to take a vow to practice nonviolence. Sometimes I will read a doha, a song of realization, from Shabkar in which he describes how to meditate in Dzogchen. He instructs us that the way to awakening in Dzogchen is through sitting in silence. I always get happy whenever I read that doha. My heart just cracks open at his words.

One time, I was translating Shabkar's text, *The Flight of Garuda*. At that time, there was a lot of chaos happening in the world along with a cycle of news that had a strong emotional impact on many of us. I remember that the moment I started translating the text, the people I was working with suddenly seemed happy. Someone else overheard me translating and told me that she also got happy just hearing the words of Dzogchen. I realized that these things are not that abstract after all, and they really do help people see a bigger reality, one where we can see the whole picture and not get stuck in the nitty-gritty drama of the mundane world.

The end of this verse has the aspiration to find an unshakeable ground in that union, which is the true awakening. The ending line reminds us that this is not just a philosophical text but a prayer inviting us to hold that aspiration wholeheartedly. So one can read this doha as a philosophical text, meditation guidance, and also as a prayer.

VERSE 9 - THE SPONTANEOUSLY PRESENT STATE

The meaning of the Great Middle Way—non-abiding.
The nature of Mahamudra—all-encompassing and
spontaneously pervasive.
The vital point of Dzogchen—liberation from extremes
and expansive.
The qualities of the bhumis and path are complete within
ground—within the spontaneously present state.
May I reach the citadel of the king of all fruitions.

Madhyamaka, or the Middle Way, is the ultimate truth in the sutras. In the *shastras,* the commentaries on the sutras, especially commentaries on the *Prajnaparamita Sutras*, such as the writing of Nagarjuna, the ultimate truth is also referred to as the Middle Way or Madhyamaka. Madhyamaka is also the same as the ultimate truth in the systems of Mahamudra as well as Dzogchen. In this verse, "Great Middle Way," or Madhyamaka, does not refer to the philosophical system called Madhyamaka but instead means the truth that the philosophical system is attempting to point out.

Madhyamaka, literally *Middle Way*, means the truth that does not fall into any *ta (W. mtha')*, conceptual extremes. In general, the conceptual extremes can be categorized into nihilism and eternalism. But these are very general categories, and there is a danger that people might think all other belief systems or assertions are not those extremes. Then people would somehow validate all their own notions of reality and never question them. The moment we bring our ideas and concepts under the umbrella of these categories, we can inquire into their validity, and we will come to the realization that they have holes.

Usually in Buddhist philosophy, eternalism is believing in a theistic creator, and nihilism is denying law of cause and effect. Therefore, many Buddhist thinkers don't tend to associate most of their own ideas and beliefs with nihilism or eternalism. But from the point of view of Madhyamaka, our usual notion of reality easily falls into one of those two conceptual extremes. This can be quite shocking. It means that almost all notions of reality are false in the ultimate sense, even though they might have their own relative truth. In the ultimate sense, they are all equally bound to collapse if they are investigated thoroughly with logic of Madhyamaka. They are just mental constructs, and they cannot capture the ultimate truth, dharmadhatu, or nonduality.

One method that can help us to see how easily all our concepts and beliefs fall into the two extremes is to divide nihilism into gross and subtle nihilism, and eternalism into gross and subtle eternalism. *Gross* means it is easy to figure out, and *subtle* means it is hard to figure out.

The example used for gross nihilism is denial of cause and effect. That's easy to understand, because it is a blunt rejection of reality. But there is also subtle nihilism. If someone rejects emptiness, that is a subtle form of nihilism, because nihilism means rejecting something that is true. Usually, we may not think that rejecting emptiness is nihilism or that rejecting no-self is nihilism. It is very subtle because neurologically, it is not the way we think. It requires a very fine inquiry to figure out subtle nihilism. You can use an axe if you chop a tree, but if you want to cut a flower for your vase, you need a finer tool. Just like that, the subtler nihilism gets, the finer the inquiry that is needed to uncover it. Yet our human mind has difficulty capturing the subtleties of anything.

Eternalism can also be categorized as gross and subtle. The gross form is belief in a god, creator, or personal savior. That is gross eternalism, because if we make anything into some "thing" and reify it, then even tathagatagarbha and emptiness could be turned into forms of eternalism. The notion of tathagatagarbha, or emptiness itself, is not eternalism and transcends all conceptual extremes. Yet through our human habit, it is easy to reify emptiness, which is kind of laughable because the point of emptiness is not to reify. Therefore, this kind of caution is needed so that emptiness is not turned into some kind of quasi-religious, theistic supreme being to be worshipped and placed on a high pedestal.

Here, the ultimate truth is Madhyamaka, which does not abide in any conceptual extremes. This is called the state of non-abiding. But even the term *Middle Way* is very tricky, because it gives the notion that something stands between eternalism and nihilism, some "thing" that is independent and discrete. This is why it is said in the *Samadhi Raja Sutra,*

> *… the intelligent ones let go of all conceptual extremes.*
> *They do not even reside in the middle.*

Even the term *Middle Way* itself is not complete. Any term we use to describe the ultimate truth would never be completely perfect. No perfect metaphor, simile, or analogy can express it. All these words and concepts pointing out the ultimate truth are like the finger pointing to the moon. They are not useless, because they can help us awaken to the ultimate truth. But sometimes a dreadful tragedy happens, which is that a person sees a finger pointing to the moon, but the person ends up thinking that the finger is what is being pointed out. This kind of unfortunate philosophical tragedy happens more often than we think.

The conceptual extremes, or *ta,* are not just our unexamined notion of reality in everyday life but are also the philosophies and doctrines that are institutionally established and held by masses of followers. For example, the system known as Madhyamaka Prasangika, developed in the Mahayana tradition, does not postulate ultimate truth by making assertions but by falsifying and repudiating all philosophical tenets. Nagarjuna and his followers, such as Chandrakirti, all wrote texts expounding Madhyamaka Prasangika. They not only refuted non-Buddhists tenets like Charvaka and Samkhya but also refuted the doctrines of other Buddhist schools of thought, such as Chittamatra, the Mind-Only school. In their mind, all the schools of thought had elements of realism, because they all believed in something as ultimately real.

In this verse, the term "Great Middle Way" (Great Madhyamaka) has a very specific meaning and is not simply praise. It is not just a way to proclaim that Madhyamaka is great or exalted. The meaning indicates that this Madhyamaka is not just a philosophical construct. It transcends all assertions and is also known as the great emptiness.

For example, even though *emptiness* and *great emptiness* are synonyms, now and then you will find that Buddhist masters make a distinction between them as a way to point out that emptiness is more than negation. Great emptiness is a nondual truth that transcends all assertions, whereas sometimes emptiness could be understood as just negation, negating *svabhava*, the intrinsic nature of all things, or negating the true existence of all things.

This is not to say such a process of negation is useless. In reality, everything is our mental projection. Even mind itself is not as real as it appears. Sometimes this negation is a way to get to true nonduality. Here the term *nonduality* refers to *trö drel* (W. *spros bral*), freedom from all conceptual elaborations, which is the great emptiness, *mahashunyata*. *Great* means transcending all philosophical assertions. The absolute truth can never be said in words or understood through any concept, no matter how profound or sublime that concept might be. This nonconceptual understanding of emptiness is not always taught in other Mahayana Buddhist traditions, but it is taught in the Nyingma as well as Kagyu traditions.

Similarly, the Great Madhyamaka is not just negating nihilism or eternalism. It is more than that. The Great Madhyamaka can never be understood by the intellect. It goes beyond all words and concepts. And yet it can be realized. It is not some kind of thing that has attributes or characteristics that the mind can hold onto or play with. Yet it is not nothingness, devoid of any meaning. Instead, it is the underlying reality that one can experience vividly, in the same way one can taste the sweetness of honey or enjoy the sound of someone playing the guitar.

So here, Madhyamaka is just another name for the ultimate truth that transcends all concepts and ideas that we can imagine in the realm of possibility. Then the question is, how can we experience it? When you are in deep meditation, or when some inner opening happens in you, you can experience Madhyamaka directly. It is no longer just another profound theory, but it is a living truth that you can experience.

Therefore, the true Madhyamaka is the ungraspable, undefinable truth that you can experience in the realm of the now. But you do not experience it through having a notion of Madhyamaka that you are meditating on. That meditation still has a subtle concept of Madhyamaka, no matter how profound it might be. Instead, the true meditation on Madhyamaka is when there is no more reference point, not even Madhyamaka, and you are no longer using your mind to comprehend it. You are experiencing reality not through the thinking mind but by letting your whole being naturally experience reality on its own. Basically, the meditation is letting go of the entire structure of "me" and "my mind" trying to figure or understand something, trying to unravel some puzzle. The whole effort stops.

This is the true Madhyamaka, which is expressed in Nagarjuna's writings as well as those of Atisha. These two are both regarded as the ultimate Madhyamaka masters by Tibetans. But some Tibetan scholars tend to interpret the writings in a way that works with their own paradigm; for example, by stating that emptiness is something that can be captured by our intellect.

This verse in Jigme Lingpa's doha brings together the three systems of Madhyamaka, Mahamudra, and Dzogchen. It is saying that the ultimate truth mentioned in the sutras and Vajrayana is the same even though it is being expressed quite differently, and even though the methods to realize it are radically different from one another. This is good news, because it doesn't work to have more than one ultimate truth. Otherwise it could not be called the "ultimate" truth.

There may have been beliefs among Buddhists that the sutras expound an ultimate truth that is different from the ultimate truth taught in Vajrayana, because the expressions are different. Such misunderstandings occurred quite often in the old days. This is why some masters made sure to say they are all the same in their essence. Lama Mipham said,

The Great Madhyamaka, freedom from conceptual
proliferations,
and Dzogchen, the clear light,
both are the same meaning, with different names.
There is no view that is more exalted than this.

This verse is excerpted from Lama Mipham's text known as *The Beacon of Certainty (ngeshé drönmé;* W. *nges shes sgron me*), one of his most well-known books. The followers of the Nyingma school regard this as an authoritative text that defines the Nyingma school's position on Madhyamaka.

In subsequent verses, Lama Mipham talks about the difference between the systems of Madhyamaka and Vajrayana. He said that in the system of Madhyamaka, one uses analysis to arrive at the realization of, or awakening to, the ultimate truth, whereas in Vajrayana, more radical methods are used to experience the ultimate truth directly. In general, the Madhyamaka philosophical system is built on inquiries and analysis. These can be found in the works of Nagarjuna, Chandrakirti, and Shantideva as well. Inquiries are often based on negation. They will help you find the intrinsic contradictions among all the beliefs and philosophical assertions. Through seeing those contradictions, you can transcend them and arrive at a place where you see that the ultimate truth is beyond words and concepts.

"The nature of Mahamudra—all-encompassing and spontaneously pervasive."

Mahamudra refers to a system of practice or a path, as well as the ultimate truth that is experienced through such a system. It is taught in the Vajrayana tradition, especially in what is called the New Tantra in Tibetan Buddhism. Yet the term *Mahamudra* does not belong strictly to Vajrayana. It is taught in the sutras as well, though there is a little debate about this. For example, Sakya Pandita, known as one of the three Manjushri of Tibet, said, "The term *Mahamudra* does not exist in the Prajnaparamita tradition. The wisdom of Mahamudra is merely derived from *abhisheka* (empowerment)." He is saying that even the term *Mahamudra* does not exist in the sutras, and that the awakening of Mahamudra only happens in Vajrayana through abhisheka or Tantric initiation. But many Mahamudra practitioners strongly oppose this viewpoint. They state that Mahamudra is taught in both systems—sutras and tantras. In the context of Jigme Lingpa's verse that we are studying, it is not necessary to get bogged down in this philosophical debate. This verse is saying there is only one ultimate truth regardless of which philosophical system or tradition we are referring to.

Here, *Mahamudra* means the nondual awakening to the ultimate truth that pervades everything that exists from beginningless time. In Sanskrit, *mudra* means seal. For example, the Chakravartin, or universal monarch, is able to control the whole kingdom by his or her command, symbolized by their mudra, or seal. No one, such as other kings, lords, ministers, or subjects, can go beyond that command or seal. Just like that, *Mahamudra* means no phenomena can go beyond the great seal of the ultimate truth. Metaphorically speaking, everything is ruled by the great seal of the ultimate truth, everything is permeated by the ultimate truth, or the truth of Mahamudra.

Mahamudra, from the point of view of Vajrayana, is the awakening to emptiness or the nature of reality that is accompanied by *mahasukha*, great bliss. This notion of great bliss is unique to Vajrayana, and it is not spoken about in the Sutrayana tradition. Yet the experience of mahasukha is a powerful awakening that can help someone purify the subtle mental habits, or *vasanas.* The experience brings about awakening fully as well as quickly. The tantras teach that this mahasukha, or great bliss, is not the effect of any cause but resides in our being as an expression of our true nature.

There are some semantical differences in the definitions of Mahamudra from the point of view of Sutrayana and Vajrayana. But in essence, the true Mahamudra is the ultimate truth, the nature of reality, or the nature of mind. It's not some kind of separate truth that has its own characteristics. That's why the Tantric adept Indrabodhi said,

This is the ultimate suchness,
The unsurpassable wisdom vajra.
It is called Samantabhadra.
It is also called Mahamudra.
This should be understood as dharmakaya.

In this verse, Indrabodhi is saying the same thing that this verse we are commenting on states. He is saying that all the different versions of the ultimate truth taught in various systems are nothing more than synonyms, and they are all pointing to the same thing.

"The vital point of Dzogchen—liberation from extremes and expansive."

Here, this verse is once again saying that the heart of Dzogchen, which is the ultimate truth or rigpa, is *trö drel,* freedom from all conceptual elaborations. In general, Dzogchen describes the ultimate truth, or dharmadhatu, as having two qualities. The first quality is freedom from all extremes, which is nonduality, similar to the state of Madhyamaka that we talked about earlier. One thing to bear in mind is that freedom from extremes is not just a philosophical assertion but is the transcendence of all conceptual reference points.

The second quality is expansive, which is a metaphorical term. The ultimate truth is often described with similes like space, which is vast and unhindered, pervading everywhere. At the same time, it is not bound to anything. However, our mind cannot see it, so there is samsara, suffering, duality, and so forth. But the truth, or dharmadhatu, itself is already free from the very beginning. This is what the second term, *expansive*, points out.

We may wonder why Jigme Lingpa and other masters sometimes talk about these three—Madhyamaka, Mahamudra, and Dzogchen—as being totally in harmony with each other and being the same in essence. There are two reasons. One reason is that there is only one ultimate truth, whether you approach it from the point of view of the sutras or tantras, Dzogchen or Mahamudra. Another reason is that in Tibetan Buddhism, Dzogchen is not necessarily practiced by everyone. Not only that, as we mentioned earlier, there have been occasions throughout history when some Buddhist masters criticized Dzogchen and raised doubts about its authenticity, doubting the source of its lineage and doubting it as a path. This could have come from political motives or just from misunderstanding. So Jigme Lingpa and other masters made such statements in order to dispel these misunderstandings and to lead people to the understanding that all the systems are speaking the same truth.

"The qualities of the bhumis and path are complete within ground—within the spontaneously present state."

Generally speaking, Buddhism has a system that maps the progressive stages of an individual's awakening. This means that spiritual awakening can continue to mature and develop just as other things do. It does not mean that the initial awakening is flawed. Even though it is perfect, it can still grow and continue. This is quite understandable and not that abstract. It can be understood by seeing that our own spiritual practice often continues to grow. For example, we can see that by practicing love and compassion, these qualities get bigger and bigger in our consciousness as time goes by, as long as we continue on the path. The stages of awakening are a wonderful system, since it is true that our awakening goes through its own evolution as it matures, as it becomes more complete and established in our consciousness.

But sometimes people try to fit all spiritual awakening into these systematic maps, which doesn't always work with Dzogchen, where awakening can be very spontaneous. There is often a debate among Tibetans about awakening. If someone claims that they have an awakening, then a group of scholars might do a theoretical examination to see if that awakening fits into their system, and they are ready to discredit it. Having a system is good, but awakening is much more personal and dynamic, much more subjective. It would be difficult to pin it down with precision. This becomes quite an issue because many people have had awakening experiences of rigpa, but then there are philosophers who question the claims. Of course, people could make false claims, but the scholars could also be too extreme trying to pigeonhole experience into the categories defined by the maps of awakening.

In Mahayana Buddhism, the system that shows the inner evolution is known as the *bhumis*, which literally means the levels of awakening. The system postulates ten bhumis, extensively describing the stages of awakening and the powerful impact that comes along with each stage. Mahayana also has another category known as the five paths, which shows the map of the whole journey from prior to awakening through complete awakening. Vajrayana has its own system of bhumis and paths. For example, some Tantric systems assert there are twelve bhumis. Sometimes the names of the bhumis in Vajrayana are identical to the names of the bhumis mentioned in the general Mahayana tradition.

Dzogchen postulates a system of sixteen bhumis. This can give the impression that Dzogchen has very structured bhumis, almost like the system of ten bhumis from the general Mahayana tradition. But one has to bear in mind that the sixteen bhumis of Dzogchen are not such a rigid system, even though it has sixteen levels of awakening. For example, the Dzogchen Tantra known as *Self-Arising Awareness* states,

> *There is no such thing as bhumis somewhere else.*
> *The individual who sees the truth has completed all the bhumis.*

This statement indicates that not only is the very notion of bhumis transcended from the point of view of the ultimate truth but also that the bhumis are not some kind of rigid, successive progress of awakening, such as in the general Mahayana. Instead, it indicates that the bhumis can happen quickly in a short period of time. In some sense, the bhumis are happening simultaneously even though they are separate levels. There are Dzogchen masters who say there is no division in the bhumis, because awakening is complete and perfect in itself. But this does not contradict the system of sixteen levels of awakening. The categories of the sixteen bhumis indicate that awakening can mature, develop, and become more embodied, but it is very swift rather than a laborious process that drags on forever.

The way of Dzogchen is neither gradual awakening nor sudden awakening. Gradual or sudden awakening has to do with the individual. It could be gradual for one person and sudden for another. There is a notion held that if you meditate on Dzogchen, it can lead you to a true awakening immediately. Such a possibility should not be ruled out at all. But it is all up to the individual. In some sense, as a tradition, Dzogchen is inviting us to wake up right now, as soon as possible, not lingering and making all the unnecessary effort of spiritual practices, because they can sometimes be a beautiful trap that further delays one's awakening.

In general, sudden awakening is defined as an awakening that is complete, it doesn't have to mature, it is already perfect, and there is nothing to purify beyond that. There is no need to go through successive stages of the bhumis. This, for example, is the awakening of Buddha Samantabhadra, which happens in an instant, and when it happens, it is complete. All the enlightened qualities are already there. On the other hand, in the Mahayana and Vajrayana doctrines, there are attributes or qualities associated with each of the bhumis related to various levels of insight and wisdom. For example, in Mahayana texts, each of the ten bhumis is accompanied by qualities or enlightened attributes that describe the very precise nature of awakening for each bhumi. All these qualities can be synthesized into three attributes: wisdom, love, and power. As one goes from one bhumi to the next, these three increase. This verse is saying that all the qualities of the path and bhumis are already present in the primordial ground, the "spontaneously present state."

On the other hand, to make sure that awakening does not sound like it is out of reach for us, sudden awakening can also be defined as a profound awakening that happens spontaneously without too much struggle. That experience has a true impact on your life, so in that sense it doesn't have to be defined as the perfect awakening in which all your vasanas are gone. This makes sudden awakening more approachable.

This verse is also stating that the qualities of the bhumis and path are already completed within the ground. This is another profound statement that is quite unique to the Dzogchen system. It is transcending the idea that all the qualities of the bhumis—love, wisdom, powers, and so forth—are desirable siddhis, or attainments, that will be achieved as a final reward. Rather, it is stating that since they are already complete within the primordial ground, they are not to be achieved. Upon returning to the primordial ground, which is the true awakening, these noble and exalted qualities simply shine out as a natural expression of ground itself.

In other systems, there is an obvious or subtle duality between ourself and these exalted qualities, as if we are here as separate individuals, traversing the path, and eventually one after the other those exalted qualities would be achieved. It gives the sense that they are not here yet, but in the future, those qualities would manifest purely as a result of our effort; in other words, as an effect of a cause. This verse is not saying that we have already achieved them. But stating that they are already in the ground transcends any notion of achievement.

"May I reach the citadel of the king of all fruitions."

Once again, this verse ends by praying that one may arrive at the unshakeable citadel of buddhahood within ground. Such buddhahood, in this context, is often described in Dzogchen as the "king of fruitions." This denotes that this is the highest level of enlightenment, not just in the Dzogchen system but in the entire system of sutra and tantra. This is also simply stating that one can reach the highest level of enlightenment through the path of Dzogchen. It also indicates that the highest level of enlightenment would not be reached through some other systems if they are based too much on concepts and complex techniques.

It seems that all these different systems have their own way of describing enlightenment, even though the essence of the definitions should be harmonious with each other. In Dzogchen, enlightenment is about returning to the primordial ground. This is sometimes called being liberated in the "womb of the precious, spontaneous presence."

This is the last verse of the aspiration prayer, which ends with this aspiration for the great fruition, or enlightenment. These nine verses completely encapsulate the Dzogchen teachings. Nothing has been missed.

Colophon

The quintessence of enlightened mind, the profound seal of the great expanse,
concludes with this profound aspiration prayer.
The guardian of the teachings, the sage Rahula,
appeared in the form of a monk, and at his request, it was composed.
In order to benefit others by spreading its profound meaning,
and to complete the auspicious interdependence and aspirations,
to the one who was blessed by Namkhi Nyingpo,
the hidden Vidyadhara, the crazy one from Kong-po,
I opened this profound seal and entrusted him with it.
May its benefit for others become as vast as space.

This prayer by Jigme Lingpa is considered a terma, as we said earlier. It belongs to a particular category of terma known as mind treasure, or *gong ter* (W. *dgongs gter).* In general, the entire Longchen Nyingthig tradition is regarded as gong ter. Here, mind does not refer to the usual mind but to the enlightened or dharmakaya mind. Mind treasure is considered by some to be the highest level of terma because it comes from the most sublime source.

This short but profound aspiration prayer has a story behind the way it came into being. It is said that Jigme Lingpa had a vision of Rahula, one of the three main *dharmapalas*, or dharma guardians, of the Nyingma tradition. Rahula appeared in the form of a monk and requested Jigme Lingpa to reveal this prayer. Out of that request, Jigme Lingpa revealed this from the highest source, the enlightened mind. He entrusted this teaching to his disciple, who he refers to as the madman, or hidden yogi, of the Kong-po region. *Hidden yogi* means someone who is awakened but does not show off his awakening to the outside world. A madman, or "crazy one" is similar to an *avadhut*, one who is liberated but not bound by conventional rules. The title *madman* is often used to refer to some Tibetan yogis. Most probably, this is an individual who is referred to in Jigme Lingpa's writings as Pawo'i Wangchuk (W. *dpa' bo'i dbang phyug*). Jigme Lingpa must hold him in high regard, as the line states that this individual was blessed by the Bhikshu Namkhi Nyingpo, who is one of the twenty-five disciples of Padmasambhava.

Then Jigme Lingpa makes a prayer that not only this doha but the Dzogchen teachings in general will have longevity in this world, continuously reaching the hearts of many individuals and helping them discover the highest liberation.

Living Dzogchen

This aspiration prayer by Jigme Lingpa thoroughly covers the entire system of Dzogchen. It allows people to have a full comprehension of Dzogchen, including its philosophy. In essence, Dzogchen is a practice but it also has an unbelievably rich and sometimes intricate philosophy. This aspiration prayer is written in both *pandita* style and *kusali* style. The first is scholarly and the second is more experiential. This short prayer, if one studies it fully, allows one to get quite a detailed picture of Dzogchen from a more philosophical point of view. It also has a flavor that can lead someone to experience rigpa or primordial ground in the realm of now.

It is not sufficient to merely understand the ground, path, and fruition of Dzogchen philosophically, otherwise they can remain as just intellectual information in one's head. The main point is to actually live it. That is also the message of this prayer. If you look at the text, you see that each verse ends with a prayer, an aspiration to embody and live the message of Dzogchen in the realm of now, in daily life.

Dzogchen, in the end, is a practice that one could dedicate one's whole lifetime to. At the same time, it does not have to be a linear path. The very goal of the practice can manifest at any given moment. It's not based on a strict model of a means and a goal as separate principles nor does it have a very strict linear order and a timeline when the goal would be achieved after the right amount of effort.

According to Dzogchen, liberation, or nirvana, is really a state of your own mind that can take place at any given moment in the realm of rigpa. The impact is not mental or conceptual but can immediately pull us away from what I call the matrix of duality. This expression was inspired by the movie *The Matrix*. If you ever watched the first movie in the series, you know that the matrix is basically a world where everyone was enslaved by artificial intelligence, and people were living an illusion, thinking they were having a life while they were really being used to feed that artificial intelligence. There was an underground movement where people woke up, knew that everyone was being enslaved, and then resisted it. I found the matrix is a powerful analogy to describe the world of illusion, the duality we are completely trapped in.

In the matrix of duality, there is "me" who is separate from the totality. There is "my" life, and other people "I" either like or dislike, and "I" have all these goals for achievement, wanting love, approval, comfort and so forth. There is "me" who is competing with other people to get ahead of the game. There is fear with all that—not achieving what I want, fear of rejection and failure, and all kinds of ideas of right and wrong to get attached to. All the time, this sense of "me" or "I" is always striving towards something, holding this life together, and always fighting, even unconsciously, to control reality, to mold it into "my" preference. It is always happening. Even if we do spiritual practices, we are operating in that matrix. There is a "me" who is a spiritual being wanting to get somewhere, chasing after the big nirvana, and carrying guilt and pride. At the same time, no matter how powerful the matrix is, it can be interrupted by returning to rigpa, which is the ground of our consciousness.

Dzogchen is perhaps the most powerful way we pull back completely from that matrix. We let go of the whole thing, which results in an unbelievable sense of being free and liberated, with the realization that the truth has been there all along, regardless of what we call it—primordial ground, dharmakaya. This is Dzogchen liberation, which we can experience in everyday life, regardless of where we are and whatever we might be doing. In some sense, we can train our mind to relax in that state—the primordial ground, the dharmakaya zone—which is outside of the matrix or empire of duality.

This is why the traditional Dzogchen texts invite us to periodically go into retreat to practice the art of non-doing. The texts provide very specific instructions how to do that, such as letting go of what are known as the nine-fold activities, *jawa gu truk* (W. *bya ba dgu phrugs*). These are the outer, inner, and secret activities of the body; the outer, inner, and secret activities of speech; and the outer, inner, and secret activities of the mind. These activities encompass almost everything we do in life, whether spiritual or ordinary. But they are often motivated by our ego, either the mundane ego or the spiritual ego. This is why even certain spiritual activities can sometimes be part of the matrix as well. It might be useful here to explain the list of nine-fold activities.

The outer activities of the body are the daily chores and all the things we do in our daily life, like working at the office, putting on makeup, fixing up the garden, and so forth. All the things we do with our body. The inner activities of the body are more religious practices, such as prostrations or circumambulations around sacred statues or images. Secret activities of the body are performing esoteric practices, such as Tantric mudras and vajra dances. Outer activities of speech are talking, gossiping, and the usual chatting. Inner activities of speech are reciting prayers and liturgies. Secret activities of speech are recitations of mantras or names of the deity, or *ishta devata,* as part of Tantric sadhanas. The outer activities of the mind are just ordinary mental activities, such as thinking, ruminating, fantasizing, and so forth. Inner activities of the mind are reflection, spiritual inquiry, or study of sacred doctrines. The secret activities of the mind are like Tantric practices, such as the creation of the mandala in one's mind.

In some retreats, we are encouraged to let go of the nine-fold activities, because all these activities can sometimes be a part of the matrix of duality. Dropping them allows us to pull our consciousness away from duality and just rest in the primordial ground of all things, where we experience a state of mind that is not the show of the ego, but something that is much more spacious or profound—rigpa, or dharmakaya mind.

This does not mean that you should not do other practices, such as mantra recitation and mudras, when you do Dzogchen. It just means that now and then it would be very powerful to let it all go, whether for a whole week or part of the day. Again, it doesn't mean that you should not do all these spiritual practices when you do Dzogchen. This is a vital point that people should not misunderstand. That could be a serious misunderstanding.

But either on retreat or in everyday life, let the matrix collapse so you feel the extraordinary freedom that is already there. Then all your struggles go away naturally. By doing this, eventually our whole consciousness becomes more in tune with rigpa rather than with the matrix of duality. There is a benefit to be reaped from doing this. We will begin to find an unconditional happiness through which we can be quite grounded and happy regardless of what conditions are taking place in life. This is why some Dzogchen masters use the expression, "The sun of happiness shines from within." This expression describes a happiness that comes from a deep place, from being free of the matrix and no longer dependent on any outer circumstances.

Dzogchen often uses a lot of terms such as resting, relaxing, or letting yourself fall into the nature of mind. These expressions are reminding us that in the end, there is nothing to be done. We don't have to do anything. We don't have to strive to get to inner freedom. Instead, there is a way we can simply and immediately drop everything and just rest in it.

For example, some of the Dzogchen masters talk about using simple yet effective methods to immediately, in a single moment, drop into that state, which we are calling dharmakaya or primordial ground. Earlier, we described one example from the well-known text *The Three Words of Prahevajra* by Patrul Rinpoche, which talks about using the exclamation of the *Phat* syllable to immediately shock your thinking mind. The matrix just collapses in that single moment, and you discover you are already resting in awareness.

Other methods include gazing into space or sitting in a certain meditation posture known as *sem nyid ngel sö chak gya* (W. *sems nyid ngal gso'i phyag rgya*), which means resting in the nature of mind. The posture or mudra is sitting down, resting your hands on your knees. For example, the iconography of Longchenpa shows him in a relaxing meditation posture with this particular mudra. Even his image could be a wonderful catalyst to remind us to relax and be at ease.

Recognizing thought as thought is also our practice. In the end, this is what Dzogchen is. The moment you recognize thought as thought, there is no more unawareness. Can you see that in such simple recognition, you discontinue the very old habit of totally believing your mind? In Dzogchen, there is a famous saying which goes, "the more kleshas, the more dharmakaya." This perhaps sounds very contradictory, but it does not literally mean that we should try to have more kleshas. It is a humorous logic, which means that whenever you recognize thought as thought, and you are not lost in it, there is liberation, there is awareness right there, which is referred to as dharmakaya.

The saying also reminds us that in Dzogchen, with awareness, our kleshas do not have to be rejected. They will be liberated on their own in the realm of awareness. There is a term known as ordinary kleshas, which is experiencing our kleshas without any awareness. In such a moment, kleshas become ordinary and basically bind us. Whereas, as long as there is awareness, even though kleshas might arise, they do not bind us inside.

There are other specific practices that can be integrated into your daily life in order to live Dzogchen. One of them is reciting or chanting a really rich Dzogchen text that would remind you to drop into rigpa, such as Longchenpa's *Dharmadhatu Kosha (Chos Ying Dzod* in Tibetan); the Dzogchen aspiration prayer by Lama Mipham; and this very prayer by Jigme Lingpa, which is often considered the most important liturgy chanted in the Nyingma tradition.

All these simple gestures and practices can take you immediately to that dharmakaya state. So the way we live Dzogchen is not by walking a linear path with a result in the distant future. It is experiencing liberation in everyday life. This is how one should practice Dzogchen, and this is the invitation from the great masters of the past.

My wish is that many people will find this prayer to be a compass for everyday life that points them to the ineffable, as expressed in the colophon: "May its benefit for others become as vast as space." My aspiration is that this commentary will help people have a deeper understanding of this precious prayer.

I shall pray that the precious teachings of the Dzogchen masters like Jigme Lingpa may shine like the brilliant sun in the sky and illuminate the minds and hearts of many. Through that, may many experience the sun of happiness shining from within.

About the Author

Anam Thubten grew up in Tibet and at an early age began to practice in the Nyingma tradition of Tibetan Buddhism. He is the founder and spiritual advisor of Dharmata Foundation and teaches widely in the United States and abroad. More information about Anam Thubten, including his teaching calendar, can be found online at dharmata.org.

Anam Thubten's published books in English and other languages include:

No Self, No Problem;
The Magic of Awareness;
Embracing Each Moment: A Guide to the Awakened Life;
Fragrance of Emptiness: A Commentary on the Heart Sutra;
A Sacred Compass: Navigating Life Through the Bardo Teachings;
Choosing Compassion: How to be of Benefit in a World that Needs Our Love.

www.ingramcontent.com/pod-product-compliance
Ingram Content Group UK Ltd.
Pitfield, Milton Keynes, MK11 3LW, UK
UKHW020132250726
13967UKWH00002B/613